THE ENVIRONMENT
and the
AMERICAN EXPERIENCE

Kennikat Press
National University Publications
Series in American Studies

General Editor
James P. Shenton
Professor of History, Columbia University

DONALD W. WHISENHUNT

THE ENVIRONMENT
and the
AMERICAN EXPERIENCE

A Historian Looks at the
Ecological Crisis

NATIONAL UNIVERSITY PUBLICATIONS
KENNIKAT PRESS • 1974
PORT WASHINGTON, N. Y. • LONDON

For Betsy,
who really cares

Published by
Kennikat Press Corp.
Port Washington, N.Y./London

Library of Congress Cataloging in Publication Data

Whisenhunt, Donald W.
      The environment and the American experience.

      (Kennikat Press national university publications.
Series in American studies)
      Includes bibliographical references.
      1. Human ecology - - United States - - Public opinion - -
History.   2. United States - - Civilization - - History.
I.   Title.
GF503.W49   301.31'0973   74-80068
ISBN 0-8046-9071-5

PREFACE

Today there is great concern about the quality of the environment. The crisis has reached such proportions that we are warned by experts that within one generation or less the air will be too fouled to breathe, the water too polluted to drink, and the population so great that only standing room will be left. Whether these warnings are overstated only time will tell; yet there seems to be a consensus that a serious problem exists.

Faced with this crisis, we hear several questions. "Why has such a situation developed in a nation like this?" "Why was something not done in the past to prevent such a state of affairs?" "Why can't a nation with such enormous resources and with such a record of achievement solve something as simple as environmental destruction?"

Perhaps there lies the crux of the problem. Environmental deterioration is not a simple matter; it is the result of quite a complex interweaving of history. Our philosophy, our religion, our political and economic systems have all contributed to the creation of the present condition; they also mitigate against an easy solution.

One of the most astounding things one finds in discussions of current problems is a remarkable lack of knowledge about the past. Some people seem to think that the environment has been fouled in just the past few years; others suggest causes from the past that do not truly reflect history.

The goal of this book is to attempt to set the record straight. Our historic attitude toward the world around us is not some mysterious labyrinth of deviousness. An understanding of the Western tradition, especially America's role and place in that tradition, will make it abundantly clear that our present circumstances are the logical result of views we have held for at least four hundred years, and maybe more.

The idea for this book originated almost three years ago when I was asked to write an article for a college newspaper. At that time I was introduced to the writings of Lynn White, Jr., to whom I owe a great deal for stimulating my own thoughts. A special note of thanks must go to Cornell Jaray of Kennikat Press, who approved my ideas in a very rough form and encouraged me to complete the manuscript. Student assistants in the history department of Thiel College, Anita Genger and Thomas Scabareti, were very helpful in proofreading and limited research assistance. Professor Evelyn Baer of Thiel College read the entire manuscript and made valuable suggestions. The errors, however, are mine, not hers.

As is so often the case in lists of acknowledgments, special appreciation is due to my wife Betsy. It was she who first stimulated my interest and concern in the quality of the environment and who got us both involved in a local recycling project. In addition, she arranged our home lives so that I could be as free as possible to write this book. For these and many more things, I feel quite fortunate. The dedication of this book to her is small reward indeed.

DONALD W. WHISENHUNT

Portales, N.M.
September, 1973

CONTENTS

1

THE PROBLEM

Anyone who is unaware of the current concern over the environment must truly have been living on the moon or at some remote outpost during the past several years. To some, protection of the environment has become the latest cause, a suggestion of a movement that takes on the nature of a crusade. The public often reacts negatively to a crusade out of fear that the supporters may well be idealists who are often little more than troublemakers.

Reform efforts have always been a common feature of American life. Many movements demanding change of one sort or another have come and gone, some with complete or qualified success and others with dismal failure. Studies of past movements do not offer any meaningful suggestions as to the causes of failure. To model a current movement after one in the past, with the hope of avoiding previous mistakes, is to court disaster, since no two periods are similar enough to suggest duplicate results. Often the supporter of causes—the reformer in the most pejorative sense—has been dismissed as an idealist, a crank, or a malcontent, unwilling to accept the advantages of modern society even though it may be less than perfect. For some, environmentalists appear to be merely the latest in this long line of sincere but misdirected do-gooders.

Anyone who decides to become a champion of the environment must recognize that he will meet much opposition. For those who are comfortable with the status quo, the mere suggestion of change will undoubtedly be frightening. This is even more true when the recommended change confronts and challenges long-held views based upon one's religious, economic, and social heritage. Anyone who wants to change those values seems to be a social tinkerer who offers more of a threat than an improvement. Moreover, a reformer, finding power marshaled against him, may see his movement aborted, diverted, or stopped before he realizes what has happened. Events of the recent past provide good examples of this potential.

During the sixties the United States was subject to at least three major movements that achieved varying degrees of success. Numerous other smaller or aborted ones also appeared briefly and then disappeared. The decade opened with the civil rights movement. An attempt by both blacks and whites to redress injustices of at least a hundred years duration, the movement went through several phases. After the first efforts of blacks to assert themselves in the fifties began to get sympathetic attention, whites began to join the effort in the early sixties. During this highly idealistic phase joint cooperation between the races to break down the legal and social barriers to equality seemed to be achieving some success. The most hopeful period came with the passage of the landmark Civil Rights Act of 1964, but in retrospect that seems to have been the high point of optimism and interracial cooperation. Thereafter divisions began to appear. Suspicion of the motives of white liberals, the failure of massive federal legislation to correct immediately the long-standing injustices, and the rise of violence from both sides, culminating especially in the deaths of leaders like Malcolm X and Martin Luther King, Jr., all helped to destroy the movement that only a few years earlier offered such hope of successfully eradicating barriers to racial harmony. In the late sixties the black movement took on different attitudes, and its leadership was scattered. At decade's end the future of what few would any longer call the civil rights movement was very unclear.

The Vietnam war had a major disruptive impact on the civil rights movement and in creating the second major movement of the decade. Martin Luther King's joining the antiwar protest in his later years helped to alienate some white liberal supporters who were still caught up in the Cold War mentality of the fifties and supported American efforts in Southeast Asia. Riots and other violence, along with the growing hostility of blacks, helped to drive away other white supporters. Gradually, as the decade came to an end, white participation in civil rights activity virtually ceased. Additionally, the objectives of black organizations changed dramatically from integration to black separatism and black political control of their own communities.

As American involvement in Vietnam increased, a very active and militant protest against it gained momentum in this country. Antiwar activity eventually became the second great movement of the decade. Very unacceptable to most of the population throughout the war years, the antiwar activists took many personal risks. They were branded as disloyal by many of the supporters of the war, and some even suffered personal attack and abuse for their efforts. More than ever before in our history young men went to prison rather than submit to the draft, fled to Canada to avoid the military service, or became deserters after induction. Although the majority of Americans never approved of these more extreme actions, they did become sympathetic, as the war continued year after year, to American withdrawal from the conflict. With the recent signing of a peace agreement in Vietnam, many now predict that the antiwar movement will end.

Some of the more cynical blacks voiced the opinion that the intensified war effort in Vietnam was a deliberate attempt by the government to end internal divisions. Experiences in past wars revealed that in a time of national emergency a degree of internal unity was achieved that could never be maintained in peacetime. They believed, therefore, that part of the reason for Vietnamese escalation was to divert American attention away from civil rights and to blur the social divisions that existed at home. If true, it was a serious and costly price to pay for a questionable objective. It is true, nonetheless, that many of the young who had been major participants in the civil rights movement moved now to antiwar protest, and the agitation for black rights and identity were either ignored or moved down on the list of priorities.

Some of those who believed that the government deliberately distracted the civil rights movement also believed, to a certain extent, that the third major movement of the decade—environmental protection—was another attempt of the government to deflect youth participation from what it considered an undesirable activity—in this instance, antiwar protest. They claimed that the environmental movement was a phony issue created by the power structure only to defuse the antiwar protest and that the danger to the environment was grossly overstated.

There are certain basic weaknesses in the claim that the government was deliberately manipulating thought and action. First is the assumption that the federal government was not committed to the goals of civil rights. Without question, there were many bureaucratic officials who did not support it, but it is likewise true that the full power of the presidency of Lyndon Johnson was behind the movement, even to the extent of forcing through Congress three major pieces of civil rights legislation with more sweeping powers than any in the past one hundred years.

Second, if we assume that the president and white liberals were soft in their support of a racial justice which would dramatically alter the status quo, it is the ultimate in cynicism to assume that they would start a major international war with all its potential consequences just to blunt a domestic movement. Third, it is even more unreasonable to assume that the war would have continued after it created such serious internal social upheaval if its only purpose had been to destroy civil rights activity.

Furthermore, the choice of environmental protection as a diverting "cause" would have been a poor choice, since the potential for upsetting the status quo was even more far-reaching should the movement catch hold and be carried to its ultimate conclusion. It seems more logical to assume that each movement was indigenous and spontaneous to a greater degree than most people suspect.

If one looks realistically at the current situation, the threat to the environment is obvious. There is little need to recount the environmental destruction that goes on every day even in the most remote parts of the country. Urban dwellers may be most aware of the dangers because of air and noise pollution and the massive destruction of waterways, once beautiful streams, that have become open sewers today and even, in some places, occasionally catch fire. But even the residents in rural regions have witnessed the destruction of forests, the disappearance of wild game and fish, and the increasing atmospheric haze which was not there only a few years ago.

Virtually all the media bombard us daily with reports on the extent of the problem. This not only includes the gradual physical destruction of the environment through careless and ceaseless exploitation, but it also includes peculiarly modern crises that are a result of careless use of natural resources. For example, we have been told for several winters that an energy crisis was on its way, and that the time would come when we would not have enough natural gas and fuel oil to operate at normal capacity. Finally, in the winter of 1972–73, this crisis developed even though it was an unusually mild winter in many parts of the country. The resources were not gone, the experts told us; they simply were not managed properly, for one reason or another, to meet the needs of an urban-industrial nation. We were told that we should have been warned a few years earlier when electric power failed altogether in New York City and the residents faced a total blackout. Again, the experts told us that there was no shortage of electrical power; the problem developed because the demand at peak periods was too great for the facilities available. Unfortunately, if this should have been a warning, reassurances from numerous public officials calmed most fears. Both these episodes, among many others, revealed that the environment is being pushed to its limit to provide for complex, modern societies.

Without question, the United States faces a serious environmental problem. The degree of its seriousness and extent must be assessed by experts who are competent in such areas, and the planning and use of these resources will have to be made on rational understanding of what the situation really is. But, at the same time, the average person has a responsibility also. He must recognize the true nature of the problem and be willing to adjust himself to the personal restrictions and limitations which will be required when we are faced with the critical condition that will undoubtedly come. Likewise, each person must do what he can to educate the public to the problem and to offer rational suggestions, in terms of both proposals and individual actions, that will help solve the problem or, at least, make its endurance more palatable.

One of the most difficult jobs the would-be reformer has is to understand the attitudes of the people who despoil the environment. Americans are not by nature evil people; they do not destroy the environment because they get some special perverse pleasure from wreaking havoc. President Lyndon Johnson made a very good point in this regard in his last public speech. Although he was speaking about racial justice, his remarks are applicable to everyone who wishes to change long-held views. He told civil rights leaders to approach those in a position to change things and ask for a hearing. But he warned them not to attack President Nixon and his administrative personnel as evil people because they do not think of themselves that way. Even if you disagree, he said, they think of themselves as good and decent people who are trying to do what is right. Therefore, to weaken your case before you start by attacking them is foolish. The same advice could be given to environmentalists. The attitudes and actions of persons in power, and of the people generally, are the results of centuries of acquired customs and habits. Therefore, to understand current problems of the environment, one must be aware of and understand the historical context from which they emerged.

For the most part, the generation that emerged in the sixties is a totally present-minded group that has little regard for the past. They consider history to be the dead hand of the past that has most often been used as a means to control their actions. Unfortunately, this attitude toward history is not necessarily limited to the young, and much of the responsibility for it must be laid at the door of American education. History has too often been taught by people who have other academic interests and who do not really understand history. It has been taught as a dry, unemotional subject that more often discourages students than it excites them. When confronted by demands to know why one should study history, too many teachers have retreated into the ivory tower where they do not have to defend themselves. Students have been told that history must be studied because it is in the curriculum and because it is good discipline for the mind. Unfortunately, the student has been turned away from the study of a very meaningful subject just because someone has been so thoughtless as to consider his concerns unimportant.

In addition, the current generation thinks that history is used merely as a weapon by the older generation to keep them in control. It is probably true that older persons have too often used the past to threaten or intimidate the young. What young person has not been told by his parents how lucky he is to be living in this day and age when luxuries abound and sacrifice is not required? We have all been told how our parents suffered in order to attend school and about how bad things were during the depression. People using these arguments probably do not deliberately distort the past, but their mistake has been in using the lessons of history in the wrong way. Such examples imply a threat that if the young do not do as they are told, the benefits of the modern world may well be eliminated, or they are made to feel guilty for their affluence since their parents suffered so much. It is not hard to understand why the young "tune out" older people and even reach the point of totally disbelieving them. Teachers are often struck by such an attitude when they find large segments of their students who do not believe that there was really a depression at all. They have been told about it for so long that many of them conclude that it is merely a figment of their parents' imagination.

The antihistorical attitude of the modern generation is disturbing for a number of reasons. For those who have undertaken it, the study of the past is justification in itself. The satisfaction and pleasure that one receives from understanding human history is so great that the student of the past is often mystified when confronted with people who think that past events are dull and dry subjects for inquiry. But he should be more aware of popular thought and understand that, for the more utilitarian American, mere exploration of the past is not enough. The public must be shown its practical and useful nature.

Throughout the past the historian has on occasion taken note of this antihistorical view. Unfortunately, too often he weakened himself and his profession to make his work seem useful. This willingness to conform is somewhat parallel to the whole matter of American education. Classical education gave way under the pressures of newer discoveries and developments that seemed more "relevant." Education changed from training the mind to training for life to training for a job. Unfortunately, the historian is in danger of going along with this trend. He has too often reacted defensively and claimed much more for his profession than he can deliver. Many times he has offered practical or utilitarian benefits which are questionable at best. The pressures upon him are intense to explain what history is for or why it should be studied. One could take a cynical attitude and reply that if one has to ask the question, then there is no answer for it. But that is evading the question. The historian must have an answer, but it must be meaningful and realistic.

There are many possible answers to be found. George Santayana has said that a nation that will not remember its history will be condemned to relive it.[1] That may be too cute an answer, but it is one of many. Obviously, history has much to say to us today. We will not necessarily be condemned to relive it, but without knowledge of the past we may make some of the same errors that our predecessors made. Despite lingering misconceptions to the contrary, history does not repeat itself. There are parallels between different periods, to be sure, but the periods are not the same. The person who acts on the assumption that they are is asking for trouble.

It is possible for us to learn from history, however. We can study past actions and learn about the successes and failures of the past. This will not assure success for us, but it will offer some guidelines. One of the primary uses of history for the present is to give the contemporary world some understanding of the attitudes and atmosphere of the past as they affect the present. It is in this way, more than likely, that the environmentalist can learn the most that will be helpful to him.

Above all, the major benefit from the study of history is the identity it gives us. Americans are familiar with the concern about genealogy and family trees. Virtually any librarian or curator of public documents will attest to the fact that more and more people are searching for their ancestral antecedents for one reason or another. Probably affluence and increased amounts of leisure have been major contributors to this upsurge of interest. More important, however, is the desire for identity. This is, of course, a part of the larger picture of contemporary alienation and the search for identification, either individually or collectively.

Just as genealogy tells us who we are as individuals, so too does history tell us who we are collectively as a nation. Any nation that loses a sense and understanding of its past becomes a rootless nation in very great danger of disintegration. Perhaps those who are concerned about contemporary American problems would do well to have a better understanding of our past and encourage others to do the same. Page Smith[2] has explained very well how a reverence for history helps to hold a people together despite the adversity that they may face. He believes that the Jews have survived as

a people and a culture, despite persecutions and dispersion, because they retained a very strong consciousness of their past
and of their culture. By contrast, it might also be suggested
that American blacks have been weakened and disunited because the American system of slavery deliberately attempted
to destroy, successfully to a very great extent, their knowledge
of the African past and heritage. The efforts of American
blacks in the past several years to reestablish links with Africa
seem to be an attempt at cultural and racial identification similar to the efforts of Jews to preserve their links with their past.

If history is able to identify a people, then the time and
effort necessary to learn and understand it is a very small price
to pay. If we know where we came from, we are better able to
understand who we are, and, to some extent at least, why the
world is the way it is.

Among the greatest problems faced by the environmental
movement today is the tendency to view the problem totally
from the contemporary perspective. This may well be the most
serious mistake it makes. For example, there are technical experts in all fields who tell us that specific acts must be taken
to save the environment. Often these proposals involve a massive reordering of previous attitudes and actions. Such changes
will not be readily accepted, especially if the suggestions are
handled badly by the advocates of change. There are those
people, of course, who will resist the necessary changes, either
out of sheer cussedness or because they think the changes are
unnecessary and the reformers a bunch of alarmists. Various
recent efforts at ecological protection also reveal that the reformers are often rude and insensitive to the attitudes of those
who resist. Under such circumstances, ecological salvation
seems doomed to failure.

Much of the problem just detailed results, more than anything else, from the absence of a sense of history. The person
who resists environmental protection because he does not believe the changes are necessary or because he will be discom-
fited must be made aware of the past American record with
the environment as well as of the fact that there does exist

today a problem that presents a "clear and present danger." If he is made to understand that the entire American experience has been a continual exploitation and despoliation of the environment, he may well conclude that drastic action is needed to reverse trends that are three or four hundred years old.

The environmentalist too must become aware that current ecological problems are a direct result of our past and that attempts to deal with the ecological crisis in the vacuum of contemporary reference are probably doomed to failure. After all, anti-environmental actions committed every day by average citizens occur not because people are bad but because they are following behavioral patterns established generations ago that have never been questioned. A person does not easily accept being told that things he has done all his life are wrong. The story of the husband having a difficult time adjusting to the new life style forced on him by his wife's conversion to the Women's Liberation movement is a good illustration of the problem. When asked if he opposed the ideas of Women's Liberation, he explained that the changes demanded by women today were just and reasonable and should have been made years ago. When pressed further, he stated that he was bothered personally only because he was married in another era when attitudes were different. Now, he said, he had difficulty in adjusting to rules that were being changed in the middle of the game. No matter how much he agreed with the goals intellectually, the personal adjustment took much longer. For the person confronted with new environmental realities, the reaction may be much the same—a kind of cultural shock. For the environmentalist to attack people of this sort as stupid, lazy, or indifferent does not achieve much. It simply polarizes people around positions that they might not normally support if they had the chance to make a decision in a calmer atmosphere.

One of the best ways for the environmentalist to approach radical change is to be aware of historical precedent. He must understand the historical background out of which current practices arose, and he must be patient and understanding when his urgency is met with hesitation or indifference. Although a reformer likes to consider himself an activist who achieves results, many times he has to be content with playing the role of public educator.

Unfortunately, few systematic studies have been made of the historic American attitude toward the environment. We are aware of some of the destruction and exploitation, and history records some of the efforts made to conserve the environment. However, there has been no overall view of the situation. The time has come for the historian and the general public as well to look at our past in a slightly different way. Instead of studying politics, wars, treaties, and continental expansion in the same traditional ways, we need to look at our past to see if we have followed a consistent pattern of action toward the environment, to analyze the impact of such action, and, if possible, to suggest ways of correcting the improper practices.

Such an order is a tall one. This modest effort is in no way meant to be a definitive study of American history. This is merely one interpretation of our past which aims to correct and fill in some of the gaps in our previous study of history. Since the problem of total environmental protection has never before been a major public issue, historians have tended to ignore this aspect of history. Instead, they usually interpreted those issues of the past that had the most visibly direct relationship with the present. This effort is an attempt to move from the current debate about the environment back through the pages of history to see why we have reached the point where total destruction of the environment seems a distinct possibility. Hopefully, this modest effort will provoke more serious, in-depth research into our environmental past. We have a serious need to understand it more fully. If this goal is achieved, this effort will have been successful.

The ideas expounded here are not presented as original. All the historical evidence discussed is common knowledge to the historian, and most of it will be vaguely familiar to the literate reader. It has been the purpose to use well-known historical material for illustrative purposes. The goal has been to interpret a little differently what we already know about the past, not to discover new knowledge.

No solution has been offered here, either. This is no master plan or blueprint for environmental salvation. To offer solutions is not really the role of the historian. His duty is to outline the past, state the problem as he sees it, and then quietly disappear from the scene. If he does more and goes further, he is no longer a historian. What he can legitimately offer is identification of possible areas of difficulty.

The basic environmental problem is one of attitude. If all people were agreed on the seriousness of the situation and convinced that something had to be done, the problem would be close to solution. The difficulty about the environment is not only what we do to it; the larger problem is what we think about it. And what we think about it today is the result of the American experience, and in some ways, of the whole Western tradition.

In order to save the environment, ingrained attitudes toward it must be changed and redirected. And that constitutes revolution. One hestitates to use that word because it has been so overworked, but no other word or phrase seems to state the problem dramatically enough. It can be a peaceful revolution if accomplished soon enough, but if we reach the really critical point without any discernible progress, then the violence of past revolutions will seem like child's play.

This is no hysterical attempt to be dramatic. It is simply the truth as many people see it. Thus, to bring about the change as quickly as possible, attitudes must be changed even if to do so does seem radical and revolutionary.

When looking at the American past, we find four or five attitudes that have been significant in their impact on our thinking toward the environment. To change any one of them will be shattering; to change them all, as seems necessary to save the environment, will truly constitute a revolution.

2

THE INTELLECTUAL REVOLUTION

The United States, a phenomenon of modern history, is the result of many forces from the past, and of the blood, sweat, and tears of many unknown people. On the surface, the creation of an American nation was mostly a physical and political act. However, if one is to understand contemporary America, he must understand that it is also the result of the ideas and concepts that we associate with modern history.

In the realm of ideas, several concepts were instrumental in creating an American nation. The concept of change is basic to the study of history and no less to that of the United States. Very much related to change is the idea of progress. Related to both have been the traditional American optimism and faith in the future. American thought patterns are also the result of an inherent anti-intellectualism. Other intellectual characteristics undoubtedly exist in this country; an understanding of those named, however, is vital to the contemporary environmentalist.

These concepts have influenced and shaped the contemporary scene far more than one might imagine on first glance. Improvement in the environment, if that be a serious goal, must result from the understanding of and the willingness to modify or change these basic concepts. Viewing them in

14

historical context will reveal how important they have been and how fixed they are today in the American mind. The re-direction of these concepts for the purpose of environmental improvement will require nothing less than an intellectual revolution.

One of the most dynamic forces in creating an American nation was the idea of progress. Few Americans would dispute the existence of progress. We use the term every day; we act as if it has always existed and always will. We built a nation on the assumption that change occurs and that it is change for the better, i.e., progress. We probably are not consciously aware of its existence; we simply take the idea for granted.

Despite American reverence for it, the idea of progress, in historical terms, is relatively new. Not so long ago a man was born, lived, and died with little prospect of change during his lifetime. He was born into a certain social and economic class with his future already determined. The possibility of changing his position in life rarely occurred to him. Social mobility, which we accept without question in modern America, had no meaning for him. If he were born a peasant, he would always be a peasant. Physical mobility was also out of the question; to go more than a few miles from his home during his lifetime was an exception to the rule. A man simply lived as his father had before him.

Little chance was offered for improvement. He farmed the same land his father had cultivated with the same tools and techniques. He almost always lived on the borderline of famine. If the forces of nature were favorable, there was enough food for the table but little extra; if rainfall were too scarce or too plentiful, if pests were too numerous, or if the soil finally reached the point of exhaustion, the resulting crop failure caused serious human suffering.

With virtually no improvement possible in his life style, our mythical man had little incentive to improve agricultural techniques, to care for the soil properly, or to plan for the future. Increased production usually benefited only the land-lord for whom he worked.

Life expectancy for this hypothetical man was very short. Diseases were serious; epidemics were a constant threat that often materialized to the point of killing large portions of the population. Medical knowledge was primitive, to say the least; medicine, still mostly superstition, most often treated the symptom rather than the cause of illness. Treatment may well have been as bad as, if not worse than, the disease. Pioneering efforts to expand medical knowledge were often met with superstitious and religious barriers. Progress in medicine was slow at best.

Obviously, the premodern man's life was bleak. His primary ray of hope or consolation was his religion, which taught him that acceptance of his lot in life was a part of God's plan. Patient and understanding suffering in this world would be rewarded in the hereafter with those things not available in his earthly life. Under such conditions, it seems little wonder that Heaven was often discussed in terms of "streets paved with gold" or as the "land of milk and honey." Prior to the introduction of the idea of progress, man lived only slightly better than the animals that he kept to nourish himself. A society of this sort was ready for a new idea.

That new idea was "progress." To pinpoint the exact date of origin of such an idea is most difficult. Perhaps our premodern man stopped one day to question his condition in life. Perhaps he wondered why he could not live like the lord in the manor house. He may have wondered why man must wait until the hereafter to enjoy the rewards the Church promised him. He may have asked himself why man, whom the Church taught was the center of creation, should not live better than animals. On the basis of subsequent history, he and his successors must have concluded that his condition in life did not need to remain static—that it could, in truth, change for the better.

Whatever its origins, the idea of progress introduced a very revolutionary concept into human society. If a man could improve himself, it seemed only logical to assume that man is perfectible. Did not the Church teach that each man must strive to be as much like Christ as possible, always recognizing, of course, that he is mortal and cannot achieve the perfection of Christ?

The consequences of an idea like progress are nothing less than earth-shattering. In recent years the same influence has been called the "revolution of rising expectations" in the under-developed world. People in backward (i.e., nonindustrial) areas have observed developed societies through the marvels of modern communication and have asked why they should not also share in material prosperity. Is this not just an intensifica-tion or a contemporary manifestation of the idea of progress?

An example of the idea of progress in a contemporary setting is the recent black activism in the United States. Many white Americans have been mystified about why a Black Revo-lution occurred in America at all, and specifically about why it came at the time it did. What, they asked, did the blacks want? Moreover, they wondered, if blacks really believed that they were mistreated in this country, why had they not de-manded equal treatment in the 1930s or 1900 or 1880? Both these rather naive questions can be answered by an adequate understanding of history. The answer to the first question is rather simple. The thing blacks wanted was to share in the promise of America; they wanted progress for themselves. The answer to the second question is also fairly simple. Blacks did demand equality earlier. However, those speaking out were small in number and never gained the attention of the white world in any significant way.

Then why did the Black Revolution gain so much momen-tum in the 1950s and particularly in the 1960s? Part of the answer was the existence of very effective black leadership in the person of Martin Luther King, Jr., and others. But to be fair, we must remember that there were important black leaders in earlier periods, including Frederick Douglass, Booker T. Washington, W. E. B. DuBois, and Marcus Garvey. The difference in the fifties and sixties seems to be the infusion of the idea of progress within the black masses in America.

Eric Hoffer perhaps says it best: "It is not the actual

suffering but the taste of better things which excites people to revolt.''[1] In referring to those who participate in mass movements, he says, "They must also have an extravagant conception of the prospects and potentialities of the future."[2] Is he not saying that those who are willing to risk everything for change are simply admitting the possibility of progress? The average American black person probably was not willing to take to the streets to demand his rights until he saw that the possibility to achieve them existed. He saw that if he used the correct tactics, had good leadership, and was lucky, "progress" could come.

Since the dawning of modern history, the idea of progress has probably done more to change the world than any other single factor. Its impact on the black masses in America is only a very recent example of its influence. In the observance of earlier history, it seems reasonable to assume that advancement of frontiers in scientific knowledge, the age of exploration, the creation of nation states, and the Protestant Reformation would not have occurred unless the participants could see the possibility of progress.

Obviously, "progress" has many definitions. To many Europeans geographic exploration was not progress; it merely tampered with the staus quo. To the rising merchant class and to those nations that directly benefited, it was undoubtedly progress. The local nobleman who was downgraded in power probably did not view the rise of nation states as progress, but the new kings who gained power obviously did. Many Catholic churchmen did not view the expansion of scientific knowledge and the Protestant Reformation as progress. Yet all these things, among many others, introduced the idea of change and the belief that this change could be for the better, i.e., progress.

The belief in or acceptance of change is not enough in itself to explain modern history. Change alone does not offer improvement; unhappiness with one's condition is not necessarily inducement enough to bring haphazard change. People are willing to give up an old way to try something new only when they believe that improvement (progress) in one's life will result. Eric Hoffer again probably says it best, "Discontent by itself does not invariably create a desire for change."[3] Hope is the key; hope was certainly a factor in the creation of the United States.

The United States was founded and built on the idea of progress. Probably not many people actually realized that they were involved with a new idea, but they undoubtedly were. All one has to do is look at American history to see that almost everything in this country's past has been based on this idea.

Related to the idea of progress in American history is the concept of faith. In fact, the two ideas seem almost identical. The American has always believed in and accepted change; he has almost always had faith that change would be for the better (progress).

Progress, change, and faith have influenced the development of another American characteristic—optimism. Americans have always looked to the future with an optimism that at times may have been unfounded. Traditionally, we believed that problems were temporary; any unexpected difficulties would be overcome and progress would continue. Despite strong challenges, Americans most often retained their optimism. To the abolitionist the prospect of civil war may have been terrible, but its results would be worth the cost. The two world wars may have challenged optimism and faith in the future, but as a nation we committed ourselves to putting these temporary inconveniences behind us and getting on with what may be considered to be the true business of America. Some observers suggest that the Great Depression of the thirties failed to create a revolution because Americans were unable to accept the possibility that an economic system which had brought so much progress in the past could be wrong or, at least, obsolete. The depression, Americans believed, was just a temporary malfunction in an otherwise good system. With faith, optimism, and patience, the system would correct itself and America could move on to bigger and better things.[4] Later events seemed to prove the truth of the theory.

In the past twenty or thirty years, however, the American reverence for faith, optimism, and progress has ended, according to some observers. They cite growing pessimism, mounting problems, and loss of religious faith as causes. Some would have us believe that problems have become so great that most Americans despair of a solution. The validity of these claims remains to be seen. It seems reasonable, however, to assume that this will not be the case. In the past we have had dark moments, but something has always happened to restore faith and confidence in future progress.

The European who ventured out on unknown seas to discover and settle a new world in the sixteenth and seventeenth centuries did not do so just because it was fashionable. He did so with the motive of self-improvement; it might take many forms. The Jamestown colonist had hopes of emulating his Spanish brother by finding gold or other precious metals. When that failed, he turned to other enterprises, such as tobacco raising, to secure his place in the New World. The Pilgrim at Plymouth, the Puritan in Massachusetts, and the Catholic in Maryland may have come for various religious reasons, but in their own minds their lives hopefully would be better. Basic to all these colonial ventures was the idea of progress, whether it was manifested in either religious or economic terms, or in both.

The same can be said about the later immigrants to America, particularly the great numbers that came in the late nineteenth and early twentieth centuries. It is true that conditions at home in Europe made it desirable to leave. Oscar Handlin has called these the "expelling forces"[5] which cause a person to uproot himself from familiar surroundings and set off to an entirely unknown future. Handlin says that there must also be "attracting forces" pulling from the place the immigrant is going. Why did so many Europeans choose the United States over other possible destinations? Obviously, the attracting forces in America were great enough to offer hope of progress (improvement) to many people. Whether they thought of improvement in terms of economic betterment, religious freedom, lack of compulsory military service, or political rights is really immaterial. After all, each person defines progress in his own way.

A few other examples from the American past will suffice to show the pervasive influence of the idea of progress. One place where it was most completely accepted was the frontier. Since Frederick Jackson Turner called attention to the importance of the frontier in his important paper in 1893,[6] generations of American historians have studied the frontier in detail. These studies have shown, among other things, that Americans faced and conquered the frontier with a tremendous faith in the future, never doubting that progress would come. Just as the European immigrant might be hesitant to leave familiar surroundings without the hope of betterment, so too the American needed an incentive to move westward. The idea that the frontier provided a "safety valve" which drained off the discontented and prevented social upheaval in the East may be overstated; yet the West did offer improvement to those who were willing to take the risks.

It is of no significance in this context if the promises of America proved false. Even if the European became an urban slum dweller or if the frontiersman died of Indian raids or disease, he still came because of the promise of America—with the hope of progress. There were enough people, who found the promise to be true, to perpetuate the dream. Few immigrants or frontiersmen became millionaires, but for many the condition of life did improve. It improved enough to encourage others to follow after them. After all, hope (optimism?) springs eternal.

Even though Americans probably never consciously realized that the idea of progress was a basic part of our thought patterns, we have always conceived of ourselves as progressive. The nomenclature even entered into our political life. In the early part of the twentieth century, a political organization called itself the Progressive Party. Led by such men as Theodore Roosevelt and Robert LaFollette, it had the image of a political organization that moved ahead of the traditional parties to bring reform and improvement (progress) to our way of life. Parties with the name "Progressive" also made their appearances in the elections of 1924 and 1948. One may question how progressive their programs really were, but the idea of progress is certainly there.

In the 1920s a change in American schools was dubbed Progressive Education. Again the goal was to move ahead of older methods, to bring forth new ideas, to make progress. It could just as easily have been called "advanced education" or any number of other names. Yet the use of language as a symbol has always been important. Improvement to Americans means progress and vice versa. Even if Progressive Education is discredited among many educators today, the phrase does epitomize our reverence for progress.

From these few examples we can see the American reverence for progress throughout the past. In the contemporary world it has changed very little. Often the word "progress" is invoked to justify one action or another. Proponents of a freeway through a city park justify their project as progress. Opponents of the freeway who want to preserve recreational facilities or the ecological balance of the park are attacked as opponents of progress. We are told constantly that to have the benefits of a technological society, we must pay the price of progress. No matter that the price may be unbreathable air, undrinkable water, or a mounting garbage dump. After all, we cannot stand in the way of progress!

What do we really mean by the term "progress"? We may easily assume that virtually all Americans believe in progress, but does the word mean the same to each of them? Obviously not. What is progress for one man is retrogression for another. To one person progress may mean achievement of a certain quality of life, but to another it may well mean two cars for every family. Despite different definitions, it seems that historically most Americans have equated progress with greater and greater material abundance. When we speak of economic progress, we almost always mean a larger and larger gross national product and a higher standard of living geared to the quantity of consumer items we purchase. Thus, whether we fully realize it or not, for progress to continue in this country, we must continue to produce as in the past. However, each year the production must be greater because demands grow geometrically.

To perpetuate an inhabitable world and to maintain a life style with human dignity requires a serious reorientation of our values. Few Americans would argue that we have not made true progress since the first colonist landed at Jamestown. Not many would be willing to abandon the improvements or creature comforts brought by the industrial and technological revolutions. What the environmentalists seem to be saying is that enough of a good thing is enough.

The idea of progress has served America well for several centuries. But some ideas serve their time and must be discarded or overhauled in significant ways. What we must do is reevaluate the idea of progress. We must decide if we want (or can tolerate) more of what has happened in the past, or if the time has come for progress to be defined in other terms.

Shall we continue to produce new models of automobiles every year? Shall we create a demand (via advertising) for a product that no one needs? Or shall we define progress as that which provides a decent life style for as many people as possible?

To deal with our environmental problems is not just a matter of cleaning rivers or recycling glass bottles. It requires the questioning and redefining of a value system which millions of people have accepted unquestioningly for centuries. It is no small task.

For the environmentalist reformer to succeed, he must not only convince Americans to change their value system; he must also make himself acceptable to the public. How readily is the expert—in this case, the environmentalist—accepted by the general public? The environmentalist is not necessarily an intellectual by definition, but to many he is one. Intellectuals and experts—though not often the same—are often viewed by the public as the same.

Just as the environmentalist must understand the importance of the idea of progress in the past, he must also understand the pervasiveness of anti-intellectualism in the American past and present. Anti-intellectualism has been one of the strongest forces, along with progress, in the American past. Richard Hofstadter has chronicled very well the influence it has had upon American development.[7]

In the development of this nation, the intellectual always had difficulty in finding his proper niche. He never had the acceptance in America that he enjoyed in Europe. Somehow he has been suspect; his motives or reasons for existence have never been clear. The frontiersman or pioneer who met the challenge of a new environment and who survived its rigors usually felt that brawn was superior to brains. The development of the intellect, as with the growth of culture, was delayed until time and circumstances allowed it. Then, in many cases, such activities were left to the women. In a society where strength was a determining factor for survival, the intellectual seemed to be unnecessary baggage. After all, what did the person of ideas produce? Obviously, nothing tangible. Nothing that could be bought and sold in the marketplace. Thus, the person who dealt with concepts and ideas was considered little more than a parasite on society.

Only when an area became settled and achieved stability was there any place for the thinker. Only when a modicum of prosperity was achieved could he be tolerated and afforded. Moreover, it was usually the women of society who demanded education, religion, culture. Thus, in the public mind the intellectual was often associated with effeminate characteristics.

One only has to glance at a few events in our past to see that such an attitude prevailed. We always resisted cultural development; the growth and acceptance of the opera, the symphony, and the ballet have been weak at best. In times of stress, the cultural enterprises or "unnecessary frills" are the first to be restricted or eliminated.

Fundamentalist or evangelical religion has been a major

obstacle to the growth and acceptance of an intellectual community. Dealing with ideas inevitably leads to questions, doubts, and uncertainties. Many of the more fundamental Protestant faiths have resisted education for this very reason. Because of the investigation and doubts that are raised through intellectual activity, many of these groups truly believe that "a little learning can be a dangerous thing." The intellectual is a threat to the status quo in ideas, an absolute necessity to people of this persuasion. Thus, the intellectual is dangerous, perhaps even subversive.

To state the matter simply, the American people have been most reluctant to accept the advice and leadership of the intellectual. Unless he hides his abilities, he appears much too different from the average person. Although Adlai Stevenson faced many obstacles in his two presidential bids, he had to bear the additional political burden of the nickname "egghead."

In recent years the role of the intellectual in political matters has caused a reaction of blatant, open anti-intellectualism. In much of the rhetoric bureaucrats, liberals, and subversives have been equated with intellectuals. George Wallace in his 1968 presidential campaign linked all these groups together. He referred to some governmental officials as fellows "with a pointed head who can't even park a bicycle straight."[8] He later called them "pin-headed, briefcase totin', Federal harassers."[9] He also said that ". . . all those pseudo-intellectual definitions of treason and academic freedom run counter to the common sense judgment of the average man."[10] On one other occasion he referred to some newspaper editors as "know-it-alls who don't know it all."[11] One may argue that the targets of his attacks are far from being intellectuals. Yet this is obviously a neat bit of demagoguery to discredit the expert for political advantage.

A year after Governor Wallace's attacks, Vice President Spiro Agnew put it even more bluntly when he referred to "an effete corps of impudent snobs who characterize themselves as intellectuals."[12] He later referred to his opponents as "intellectual eunuchs."[13]

The anti-intellectualism is obvious in these statements. The implication is that the intellectual is incompetent to do even the simplest everyday things and he may even be a deviate. One more subtle form of anti-intellectualism was the charge made by the Goldwater forces in the 1964 election campaign against liberal (substitute intellectual) opponents that they had never met a payroll.

Some may object that these are not typical examples. It may be argued that John F. Kennedy was an intellectual who brought with him to Washington a band of bright young men with ideas. This may be true, but Kennedy did not make a display of his ability until the election was over. It should be remembered also that he only barely won election. Then, too, the Catholic issue was a major part of that election that may have made it an exception to the rule.

There are many who agree that at least one of our recent presidents was a true intellectual—Theodore Roosevelt. He seemed to be a deep and, to some extent, original thinker; he was a very prolific writer. Yet, it must also be remembered that he did his best to hide the fact. He had a public image as a cowboy, a Rough Rider, a true he-man that anyone could respect.

Perhaps one of the best examples of public distrust of an intellectual was partly the result of Roosevelt's presidency. A sometimes overlooked, yet major, part of Roosevelt's program was conservation, particularly of forest land. He used presidential power to remove enormous blocks of timberland from public use and to reserve it for national parks. He also appointed Gifford Pinchot to head the Forest Service. After Roosevelt's retirement Pinchot stayed on in the Taft administration, where he promptly ran into trouble. The famous Ballinger-Pinchot controversy revolved around the use of national forests. Pinchot said they were reserved for preservation, not for exploitation for commercial purposes. Pinchot was branded as an idealist and above all a man who stood in the way of progress. Whether this was true or not, he might well be referred to today as an "impudent snob," an intellectual.

This distrust of men of ideas has had some interesting ramifications. Since the birth of modern science, America has been deeply committed to the values of science, particularly in its technological applications. One of the simplest ways to justify an action or to make a point is to call it scientific. This sentiment also infected the academic world to the point that in the late nineteenth century we even had "scientific history."

As a nation, we admire the technician, the man who applies scientific knowledge for a specific beneficial purpose. We have little use, however, for the pure scientist who experiments and researches simply to expand human knowledge. We demand that research have utilitarian value. We honor a Louis Pasteur or a Jonas Salk, but we give short shrift to the stereotyped "nutty" professor and the "absent-minded" professor who apparently have no relationship to the real world.

The problem that we face here is complex. We value the technologist, the expert, the practical man. We somehow fear the man of ideas. Yet it would seem that an effective attempt to deal with the deteriorating environment requires not only the expert with the knowledge of how to clean the air, but also the man of deeper and more abstract ideas who can see the entire scope of the problem—one who can help us adjust to a new world and new way of life that will be required.

Yet how often in the past have we followed the advice or warnings of the man of ideas? Gifford Pinchot lost his battle, and so have countless others. We say we believe in and follow the advice of the expert. We do. We listen to the man who tells us how to raise more unneeded cotton, the man who can discover more uses for the peanut, and the man who builds a car with more horsepower. But how often do we listen to "experts" just as well qualified, or even more so, who warn us of the consequences of the technologists' advances? Very little, it seems.

Therefore, it seems imperative that we recognize the situation as it actually is. In a nation committed to "progress" and technology, the environmentalist must realize that the person who offers resistance by reminding us of the undesirable consequences of our actions will find little support. Such persons are usually categorized as "prophets of doom," pessimists, alarmists, and professional troublemakers.

The environmentalist must be fully conscious of the temperament and mentality of the American. Not only must he be fully aware of present conditions; he must also understand the contemporary world in its historical perspective. In dealing with a nation of people, he must deal with them in their own terms and within the framework of social patterns, or expect certain failure.

Thus, it would seem that a true intellectual revolution must occur if the environment is to be saved. We must decide as a nation that our definition of progress may no longer be applicable in the present world; we must convince a nation of people, without making enemies of them, that the ideas of the thinkers may also have a very important practical application. Yet at the same time this change in attitude must take place without destroying the true benefits that the idea of progress and technology have provided for us. It seems, therefore, that the promoters of the ideas of progress and technology must become responsible for their consequences. This is no mean task.

To redirect thinking in this way would be a true revolution. It would also result in serious consequences in the social, political, economic, and religious spheres.

3

THE RELIGIOUS REVOLUTION

Some professionals have suggested that the history of the United States is a history of Protestantism. Although this may be an overstatement, religion has been a major force in shaping this country's past. Religion has likewise helped mold the American's attitude toward the environment. Even though it may have as many definitions as there are people, a discussion of the environment invariably leads to man's attitude toward nature. Such a discussion may have philosophical ramifications, but it is also very much theological. The world's attitude, including the American's, toward nature is in many ways a reflection of the prevailing or dominant religious tradition. A reversal of the trends toward environmental destruction will, therefore, require a religious revolution as much as an intellectual one.

The United States, from its very first settlement, was very much in the Judeo-Christian tradition. This means, of course, that Americans have been molded in the heritage and tradition of one of the most pervasive religious traditions in the world. In modern history the Christian world has been the most dynamic and influential force in shaping the direction of the world. Therefore, the attitude of such a religious faith toward the natural world is crucial to understanding the state of the environment today. Christian nations have, by and large, been the ones to embrace industrialization most fully, and thus have contributed more than the rest of the world to destruction of the environment.

If one wishes to understand or change the American attitude which contributes to the environmental crisis, he must understand the importance of religion to American history and he must be familiar with what that religious tradition teaches about nature and the environment. The most obvious source for such information about Judeo-Christian faith is the Bible.

The Bible teaches, among other things, that man is the highest creation of God. According to the Genesis story, God spent the major part of six days creating the physical environment and the lower forms of life. The capstone of God's work was making man "in his own image." The Bible describes this act best:

> So God created man in his own image, in the image of God created he him; male and female created he them. And God blessed them, and God said unto them, Be fruitful, and multiply, and replenish the earth, and subdue it; and have dominion over the fish of the sea, and over the fowl of the air, and over every living thing that moveth upon the earth.
>
> [Genesis 1:27–28]

Without question, the impact of the ideas expressed here has been immeasurable. The nature of man has concerned people everywhere, but it has particularly vexed and agitated Americans. They have debated the exact meaning of creation "in the image of God." They have wondered if this meant a physical likeness to God or just a spiritual resemblance. Even those who said that the distinction did not matter have been very resistant, as have all Christians, to anything that would imply that such a creation story was not true.

An example of public concern and participation in this matter can be seen in the public debates about the validity of biological evolution. The basic question to most Christians, particularly the more fundamental groups, revolved around the origin of man. Did he truly evolve from a lower form—the ape perhaps—or was the Genesis account of a separate and special creation accurate? This was not merely an academic question. If biological evolution does occur—if man came from a lower animal form—then man must be demoted from his esteemed place in the Genesis story to a level with all other life forms. Christians divided over this point, with the more fundamental groups rejecting outright the evolutionary theory as directly contrary to God's word. More modernist groups varied from total acceptance to a qualified willingness to listen to differing opinion.

The climax of this controversy in the United States came for many in the famous Scopes trial—the "monkey trial"—in Dayton, Tennessee, in 1925. It was interpreted by many as a major confrontation between the forces of good, represented in the person of the Great Orator and the Great Commoner William Jennings Bryan, and the forces of evil embodied in the person of the controversial freethinker Clarence Darrow. Obviously, such an interpretation of a relatively minor event is too simple; seldom do the forces of good and evil square off to face each other in such a fashion.

Despite the ludicrous nature of the trial, many did see it as a test of man's place in nature. The trial was inconclusive; to settle such a weighty matter in a circus-like atmosphere is not easy. More than anything else, the Scopes trial provided a forum where two old rivals and antagonists could face each other for the last time. Neither side in the controversy converted the other. Fundamentalists were just as convinced afterwards that a belief in evolution was rank heresy. The liberals made the mistake of assuming that the fundamentalists were made to look foolish and that the controversy had ended. To understand the falsity of the assumption one has only to listen today to the number and variety of fundamentalist ministers on radio, particularly the Mexican border stations that beam their programming to the United States. They obviously

could not continue without listeners who are willing to contribute to their pleas for financial support.

All this has been said to emphasize how important Americans consider the place of man in the world. He is God's greatest creation, and he is free to do almost as he wishes. He controls his own destiny (within limits) and that of the world.
God is the only higher authority. Truly, man is only "a little
lower than the angels."

Again the Bible says it best:

> What is man, that thou art mindful of him? and the son
> of man, that thou visitest him? For thou hast made him a
> little lower than the angels, and hast crowned him with
> glory and honour. Thou madest him to have dominion
> over the works of thy hands; thou hast put all things
> under his feet.   [Psalms 8:4–6]

For those who accept these teachings uncritically, man is
not only God's greatest creation; he is also the center of and
the reason for creation. This view has been embodied in
Church teaching for a long time. Before the scientific revolution challenged commonly held views of the universe, the
Church taught that the earth was the center of the universe.
Man, as the highest creature on the earth, was therefore the
center of the universe.

Advances in astronomy and other scientific discoveries
undermined these teachings. Long after the Church modified
its position and sects developed with differing views, the masses
still seemed to hold to the older belief. One may argue that
such persistence is evidence only of strong egotism. However,
the newer ideas did seem to contradict Scripture, and they did
reduce man to a lower position than before. To accept such
change readily would be a great deal to ask of a simple, conservative people.

Many of the northern Europeans who settled North
America came from this religious background. They were
simple and pious people intent on doing God's will and pros-
pering while they did it. Even if they accepted the newer

scientific discoveries, as most did, they were still reluctant to lower man from his lofty position.

In a very practical sense, then, those north Europeans did not really think of man as a part of nature. He was, because of God's special favor, apart from and superior to it. The world around him was created solely for his use. God even told him that he was to have dominion over it.

From the very first Englishman at Jamestown until the present time, Americans held this view of nature and the environment. Since he was the master, he could use, modify, or manipulate the environment as he wished and as his ability would permit. Alteration or spoliation of the environment was slow at first, but as population increased and skills improved, the face of North America was dramatically changed. The greatest period of change, of course, came after the beginning of the Industrial Revolution when man learned to use machines to do his work faster and more thoroughly.

In all this development attitudes are crucial. If man was created apart from nature, the American believed he should remain apart. Through the years this separateness has increased. Contemporary Americans with air conditioning, Astrodomes, and television almost never confront nature directly. The urban dweller seldom makes contact with the natural environment. The simple act of taking a walk is sometimes startling to people who live, work, and ride in an artificial environment. The sounds, smells, and feel of nature are experienced by fewer and fewer people. Some sociologists suggest that the increasing popularity of camping and other outdoor activities is the result of a natural human desire to confront nature. One may question, however, just how serious the affluent American is in this quest. Air-conditioned campers and vacation trailers, television, and other creature comforts, all gifts of the technological revolution, offer little real contact with nature. Nevertheless, man does seem to have some innate urge to understand and to touch directly that mystical undefinable thing we call nature.

The weekend camper is only one manifestation of the

modern urge to return to nature. The creation of communes and the abandonment of the "establishment" is the other end of the spectrum. Some contemporary observers believe that this urge to nature is something new, but such an opinion only shows an ignorance or an unwillingness to understand history.

From the time Americans were able to escape nature, they began to return to it on a limited scale. Wealthy Americans have long had summer and winter homes, usually one in the city and one in the country. Others have returned to nature for philosophical or ideological reasons. The most famous of these, Henry David Thoreau, abandoned "modern" civilization in 1845 to return to nature at Walden Pond. For those interested in his motivation, he wrote extensively about his experiences. Despite his fame, one might conclude that Thoreau was not so convinced of his goals, since Walden Pond was within walking distance of town. But all these people, despite different motivations, seemed to sense that man came from nature, and they felt an unclear necessity to return to it.

American history is replete with examples of individuals and groups who found mass society distasteful enough to seek contentment in a separate environment where they were closer to nature. They range from the well-known Daniel Boone who found himself trapped by civilization when he could see the smoke from the chimneys of encroaching neighbors. Feeling cramped, he often pulled up stakes and moved farther away. Lesser known, but just as significant, groups sought in nature an escape from the sins of mass society and an environment where they could strive for perfection. Usually religiously oriented, these utopian groups often sought out nature for ill-defined reasons. Yet all these people seemed to feel an inherent urge to get closer to their origins in nature.

Such people have been judged to be malcontents and social misfits who could not get along in collective society and thus took the only alternative. They may have just not liked people. If one accepts the ideas of Robert Ardrey,[1] he may conclude that these people felt their territory was threatened by frontier expansion. Rather than stay and fight civilization, it may have seemed easier to move farther west and mark off new territory in available western land.

The contemporary American does seem to have a vague, uneasy feeling about nature. One might call it an instinct which tells man that in the beginning he really was a part of nature and that no matter how far he evolves he cannot escape his heritage. He can never move so far that he completely loses contact with his animal origin.[2] This may partly explain the weekend nature lover and the perpetuation of the nostalgic belief in rural life and values, even though most Americans do not really wish to return to the "good old days." The move to suburbia may be motivated by many things, but people often mention the advantages of living in the "country," having more space for grass and trees, and living close to nature. Thus, the American conscience causes uneasiness about our distance from the natural world, but not enough to cause great numbers to seek it out on a full-time basis.

At least two American characteristics emerge when these historical or contemporary people are analyzed. First, nature (environment or any other name one might attach to it) has been something really separate and distinct from the everyday life of the American. Direct contact with nature was to be avoided at all costs; the whole American experience has been an attempt to get away from the natural world. To create an unnatural or artificial environment is the mark of "civilization." Technology makes it possible for us today to be almost completely free of the forces of nature; we are told that it is only a matter of time until man can control nature, even to the extent of controlling the weather and producing artificial food.

Second, the American viewed nature as somehow primitive and undesirable. Although nature was a state into which man was born, it was a state from which he could evolve. The successful person—the one who had made "progress"—was the one who was as far removed from the natural environment as possible. Daniel Boone and Henry Thoreau were viewed by their contemporaries as eccentrics, perhaps even as primitives.

But today we look back upon them fondly and romanticize them as possibly the "noble savages." The contemporary hippie or other person who rejects technology and urbanization for a life in nature is also considered unusual in the pejorative sense. After all, a weekend in the woods is fine, but one does not have to go to extremes.

The conclusion that the American really holds nature in great contempt seems valid. If so, it is no wonder that he cares so little for its preservation. Nature and the environment were made for his use; if it is spoiled in the process, that is the way things are. This view is even more pervasive if it is endorsed by his religion, which is the case in Christian America.

The conclusion seems obvious that the American, nurtured in the Christian tradition, has always been out of harmony with nature. If he does not consider himself a part of the natural world, and if he spends his time trying to control it, he has little respect for it. Yet to speak of ecology implies an understanding, and implicitly, a respect for nature. Thus, for a nation steeped in a strong religious tradition, the religious leadership must recognize the crisis and modify its stand or reconcile itself to the natural calamity that faces us.

The attitude, and the scope of its significance, can be seen in specific examples. People and societies who live in harmony with nature, and as a part of it, Americans often call "primitive" or "backward." The closer a society is to nature, the more primitive it is, according to the American viewpoint. We consider progress and civilization to be measured by the distance from nature a people has moved.

Too often the American's missionary impulse has led him to make very serious mistakes in dealing with people of different cultures. Motivated by the religious imperative to proselytize, very well-meaning people have too often been condescending and patronizing. To bring Christianity and progress—often assumed to be the same thing—has most often meant that the primitive or backward people have had to give up old ways and accept modern life. Such progress often requires the separation of people from nature.

The case of the Indian-American is a good example of the American attitude toward nature. Historically, we considered the Indian-American to be backward, primitive, and savage. Over the years most people believed that to "civilize" the Indian meant to convince him to give up his old ways and move more away from nature as the Americans have.

From the first settlement, Englishmen who came to North America were unable to understand and to deal properly with the native inhabitants of this continent. True, there were examples of Anglo-Indian cooperation and understanding, such as the Pilgrim Thanksgiving episode, but the real relationship between Americans and Indians was one of hostility. American inability to get along was to a great extent the inability to understand and accept the Indian's view of nature.

The American Indian lived in almost perfect harmony with nature. This can be seen very well in the debate about utilization of the land. The American belief that the continent was virtually uninhabited is a case in point. Particularly when Americans looked at the trans-Mississippi West, they saw a vast area with unlimited potential. Yet they could see only a relative handful of native residents, who did not exploit the potential. The timber was not lumbered, the soil not cultivated, and the mineral wealth was not extracted. In truth, however, in terms of the Indian culture, the area was fully settled and the resources were used.

The basic difference between the two cultures was the view of nature. While the American lived apart from nature and attempted to dominate it, the Indian lived as a part of nature with no desire to alter the relationship that existed. The Indian lived from the bounties of nature—in fact, depended on it for all his needs—and never considered exploiting the natural wealth for so-called progress. To the Indian the deliberate destruction of the buffalo herd by American hunters was a wanton waste. The American used only the hide, but the Indian could live entirely from the animal, if necessary.

The Anglo-American concluded that the Indian was primitive and backward. Anyone who did not desire to exploit the bounties of nature, even when the potential was explained to him, must undoubtedly be very backward. Therefore, the best way to get along with the Indian was to "civilize" him by changing him to be like the white man.

The relationship between Europeans and American Indians took many forms. Those European explorers and settlers who got along best with the Indians were those from Catholic countries, particularly Spain and France. It might be argued that Protestants were least able to accept on their own terms cultures that took a basically different view of the world. The French and Spanish accepted the native inhabitants for what they were. Indeed, the French and Spanish were intent on saving the Indian's soul, but their attempts at conversion did not significantly alter the Indian's way of life. Protestant attempts to Christianize the Indians were never very serious or successful when compared to the activities of their neighbors. The French and Spanish were simply more able to adapt themselves to the Indian way of life.

A good example of the American myopia is the view we hold of the so-called Third World—particularly China and Africa. We have considered these areas to be backward and, despite much geographic diversity, similar in custom and tradition.

With the recent revival of interest in China as a result of President Nixon's visit there, some of the more sober American commentators have tried to make us realize that we have never known much about China. Even in an earlier time when we had access to the area, we cared little about the people themselves. We lumped them together and stereotyped them as quaint, barbaric, or simple. We never seemed to notice—or to care really—that Chinese civilization was a very rich culture as much as four thousand years old. Our shortsightedness was not lost on the Chinese; our boorishness, undoubtedly, influenced later developments.

Our image of Africa has been even more unrealistic.

Americans traditionally viewed the entire continent as one area populated by backward, primitive people who were all the same. We were appalled by their various religious views, their many gods, the practice of voodoo, and differing social customs. The label "dark continent" fairly well reflected the extent of our knowledge and interest. Yet only a brief study of African cosmology reveals that most African people have a highly sophisticated world-view. Admittedly, it is not in the Western tradition and is thus difficult for Western man to understand. In essence, this cosmology recognizes the importance of nature and man's place within it. It recognizes that objects do not exist accidentally; all things have a place in nature and a reason for existence. Therefore, one does not casually or lightly disrupt natural conditions by removing, altering, or modifying that object.

Americans easily become impatient with the reluctance of people of other cultures to "progress" in the Western sense. To do so would require, in many instances, the abandonment or modification of traditions, many of which are based on religious thought. Of course, Americans, according to Richard J. Walton,[3] can often see other people only through American eyes.

But America does not have a patent on progress. Change and improvement are possible in various ways. Even though progress as made by some other cultures may not be as spectacular as that in the West, it may, in many ways, be more realistic and beneficial in the long run. Therefore, to ask a people we call primitive to give up old ways, particularly those with a religious base, for a Western approach is probably asking too much, particularly when the weaknesses and flaws of Western ways become more obvious every day.

Above all, the American has never been able to see the world as others see it. Somehow, we expect the views of others to conform to our own. We have, throughout our past, accepted the fact that America has some sort of divine mission or destiny. It has been expressed in many ways—the Puritans' "Errand into the Wilderness," Jefferson's right of revolution (borrowed from John Locke) as embodied in the Declaration of Independence, the "manifest destiny" of the mid-nineteenth century, McKinley's "white man's burden," Wilson's "gunboat diplomacy." Although this concept is not specifically tied to religious views, there is a strong relationship. In a recent book on American foreign policy, Richard J. Walton says it best: "Washington has become ethnocentric and sees the whole world as an extension of itself. . . . It has come to see the United States not as one nation among many, however significant, but as *the* nation whose burdens and responsibilities and commitments can never be relinquished."[4] If America has such a destiny and plays such a major role in the affairs of the world, or if the American believes these things, then it may be too much to ask him to submit himself to the forces of nature and to live in harmony with the environment.

The American has always been mystified and most often unable to grapple with any culture outside the Western tradition. When we Americans came into contact with other cultures, we have been fascinated by them. We were curious and studied their habits. Yet we were not curious enough to study them well enough ever to really understand them. We seemed to have the idea that they were interesting, but somehow, perhaps, subhuman. If human, we certainly agreed that they were primitive. We treated them as we would children—indulgently perhaps, but ultimately firmly and paternally. Our entire relationship with the Third World has been based on these assumptions, despite the denials that come forth when the idea is mentioned.

An almost perfect example of this attitude can be seen today in our relationship with Vietnam. Critics of the American role argue that we have refused to see the Vietnam war for what it is—a civil war. They argue that we care little (if at all) for the people themselves. Defenders of our policy have constructed elaborate arguments as to our role there. That debate aside, our role in Vietnam seems to be in the classic American pattern. We treat them not as equals but as primitives who must learn from those of us in more advanced civilizations.

We are there, we say, *to protect* them from subversion, *to teach* them how to survive, *to insure* the perpetuation of democratic systems. Despite one's opinion of these goals and chances of success, the crucial issue is attitude.

Where does the American get the opinion that he somehow has the answer—that he is the holder of truth? To a very great extent, it is a result of history. The militant Protestantism which gave this country birth found it difficult to tolerate other views or dissenting opinion. Never mind that the Pilgrims or the Puritans were themselves dissenters; they dissented from untruth because they had the *real* truth. Once one has *the* truth, he cannot allow others to follow false gods. Blue laws were created and witches were attacked because they were weapons of the devil. In later years large revivals were held periodically to bring back those who had departed from the truth.

Thinking of this sort very easily infiltrates national policy. It is a feeling of superiority that is manifested in many ways. But basic to it is the absolute acceptance of the idea that man is superior and dominant on the earth. He must control it; he must not submit to it. The environment must be used, exploited, controlled. American justification for the war with Mexico in 1846 included the argument that the Mexicans and Indians resident in the Southwest did not utilize the land effectively; they were not realizing its potential. Even if the area might not generally be suitable for agriculture, it could be cultivated to some extent for a limited time. Above all, there was other potential which must not be allowed to go to waste.

Americans have apparently accepted without question the idea that man is God's highest creation and the dominant force on the earth. God told man that this was true; with his ego man quickly accepted and expanded the concept. Very easily one moves to the next step. If man is the highest creation, is there any one man or group of men that is superior to the others? Americans have unquestionably believed that they were superior to the Europe of their heritage and to the rest of the world.

In accepting and explaining this concept, Americans have joined together two world-views in a very uneasy marriage—fundamental religious faith and biological evolution, or as most commonly known in America, social Darwinism. Many fundamentalist Protestants today immediately deny such a union of ideas; yet they do seem to work in harmony at this point.

By the late nineteenth and early twentieth centuries, many Americans accepted the fact that they were the superior people (we even called ourselves a race). Fundamental Protestants could argue that this was simply God's will; God had given America a special mission. Europe was old, decayed, decadent, and corrupt. America was the hope of Christianity and Western civilization and the transmitter of its values to the uncivilized, non-Western heathen world. Thus, the missionary impulse and the imperialist zeal worked hand in hand.

However, by the latter part of the nineteenth century, Darwinism, as modified by Herbert Spencer, was a major force in American thought. Spencer concluded, and many Americans agreed, that just as biological evolution occurred among life forms, there was also social evolution. If continual conflict is a condition of nature and if the process of natural selection does truly occur, then the same sort of conflict and selection also occurs within human society. If animal life evolves, so do man, his institutions, and his society. Out of this natural social evolution, one society (or race) eventually becomes dominant. In the late nineteenth century we called it the Aryan, or Anglo-Saxon, race. Thus, to the nonreligious there was a scientific or natural explanation for America's dominant position.

The influence of such ideas was not limited to the less religious people. Not many Americans have, in fact, been truly nonreligious, and few fundamental Protestants have resisted the lure of at least some aspects of science. Thus, in the nineteenth and twentieth centuries we find moderately religious people relying on science, or social Darwinism, to explain the world while at the same time very deeply or fundamentally religious people rely on science to some extent to do the same thing. Often without realizing it, both groups speak much the same language.

Admittedly, the liberal and fundamental Protestants have very often divided into mutually hostile camps. Emotionalism and blind faith have been ridiculed by more modernist Protestants, and the fundamentalists have roundly denounced evolution and Darwinism. Yet they do have common ground on man's place in the world. Most liberals accept the existence of God and credit him with creating man and allowing him to evolve into the dominant creature. Through evolution certain groups of man (Americans, Anglo-Saxons) have evolved (progressed?) to the dominant position. Fundamentalists reject out of hand evolution and its implications. Man's position is totally the work of God. Yet they too often accept the idea of the "survival of the fittest." They may not use the phrase, knowing it is social Darwinist terminology, but other explanations often amount to the same thing. In many ways, both groups say the same thing.

These arguments lead us back to the original point. The present state of the environment must be blamed to a great extent on Christianity in its various forms. Most Christians (and those brought up in the Christian tradition or atmosphere) have accepted unquestioningly the idea that man is the highest form of creation. As such, he is not subject to the laws and restrictions placed upon other forms of life. His job is to dominate and control nature and the environment. And just look at the environment!

The salvation of the environment requires a double revolution. Not only must an intellectual revolution occur, but we must also be willing to alter radically our view of nature and man's place within it, despite the theological implications involved.

Man may well be the highest of God's creations, and he may well be the dominant species. It seems unreasonable to assume, however, that the Creator endowed man with powers far beyond other forms of life only to see man destroy himself. It seems just as reasonable to assume that man can benefit from his higher state by cooperating with nature rather than by destroying it. Man can live and work in harmony with the natural environment and enjoy a decent standard of life without destroying or radically altering conditions for generations to come. Of course, this will require a reorientation of the idea of progress, as already discussed; it will, just as well, require a theological reorientation for Americans.

To be perfectly blunt, one only has to look at the world to discover that it is Western man who abuses nature and the environment so unmercifully. It also seems no accident that the overwhelming religious orientation in the West is Christianity. Other world religions seem to have a better understanding of nature, and their teachings are more in harmony with nature. Their followers are taught that they are a part of nature.

Thus, it would follow that the real revolution must occur within the Christian world. The Christian must reassess his ego-centered world with a long-range view in mind. Understanding what has happened to nature, the environment, and the world's resources in a relatively brief time is the key to understanding what the future may be if present practices continue. Even though Christian nations may be only a small portion of the world's population, Paul Ehrlich has explained very well the excessive use of the world's resources by the very small-by-comparison industrialized world.[5] It seems an important correlation that a very large part of this small portion of the world's population is Christian or Christian-oriented.

Thus, for us to survive, the Christian faith in all its manifestations must reassess its attitude toward nature. It must decide that God did not intend for man to destroy the environment, even though he was given the power and the ability to do so. The Christian faith must realize and make it abundantly clear that man must strive to live in harmony with nature just as much as he strives to live in harmony with God. After all, if one accepts Christian teaching, nature and the environment are also God's creations. Is it not just as much a sin to destroy

God's handwork in nature as it is to destroy another of God's high creations (man)?

Such a change of views will not be easy for many Christian churches. But this is no excuse or justification for avoiding change. Christianity has had many challenges in the past, but it has survived them. Change is not easy for any institution, but when it is absolutely necessary it can be effected. For truly, a religious revolution seems imperative if man is to survive.

4

THE ECONOMIC REVOLUTION

Without question, the economic system instituted by any nation influences the way its people think about virtually everything. This is not to embrace the concept of "economic man" in the Marxian sense, but simply to realize and recognize the importance of economic concerns to virtually every individual. If the attitude about economics is so important to each individual, without question the prevailing economic system will influence the way people view and use the environment.

America, as basically a capitalist nation, has taken various attitudes toward the role of merchant, industrialist, and financier throughout its past. Never has this country been a truly capitalist nation, but the restrictions on capitalism have been minimal, and, for the lack of another term, capitalism seems best to describe our system. It is also the proper designation because the majority of the public thinks of it in this way. It matters little that the system we employ little resembles the classic definition of capitalism. The public's attitude is just as important, if not more so, as what the system really is.

American capitalism, by its very nature, is an exploitative system. It exploits for its own benefit the natural and human resources of the nation. Increasing production becomes an end in itself, because the system is based on the concept of ever-increasing production and consumption which use up the available resources. Thus, the question becomes a matter of assessing the state of the environment within the framework of the prevailing economic system. To save and preserve the environment without destroying the economic benefits that capitalism can obviously provide will require a new examination of our economic system. Such an assessment may require the abandonment of capitalism altogether or the drastic modification of it. In either instance, such a decision will, in fact, create an economic revolution.

The suggestion of a needed revision in the economic system will probably be the most controversial change required to save the environment. But it need not be. Unfortunately, in view of America's recent past, much too much emotion is involved when one discusses the relative merits of different ways of conducting the economic life of a nation. Although there are various alternative systems, the average American too often reacts to criticism of capitalism as unpatriotic. The mythology surrounding capitalism has obscured the fact that it is only one of many systems devised to conduct the economic life of a nation. In America, unfortunately, because of internal political tensions and irresponsible demagoguery, we have equated democracy with capitalism. Therefore, anyone who suggests that capitalism has its faults or that it may not be the proper system at all is branded immediately as disloyal. At that point a rational discussion of the question becomes virtually impossible.

Few people would argue that capitalism is an unsuccessful system. Through its use in this country we have created material abundance far beyond the wildest dreams of the past, despite the fact that today a greater number of people are asking if the affluence is worth the price since it has been so high, particularly in reference to the environment. Just as its benefits cannot be denied, neither can it be disputed that capitalism is an exploitative and often destructive system.

The proper approach, therefore, would seem to be a

sane, rational, and unemotional study of the system with the goals of examining its weaknesses and searching for solutions to the problems. Such an analysis is doomed from the beginning, however, if it is caught up in the emotional, patriotic fervor about "the American way."

To understand the emotional attachment of Americans to what they call capitalism, one must understand American history. Capitalism, it is said, came with the first settlers to Jamestown. The English came to the New World seeking treasure such as the Spanish had found farther south. After an unsuccessful search they eventually settled down to exploiting the other natural resources that North America offered. This wealth was not the quick riches of gold, but in the long run it offered much more potential than even the treasures of the Spanish kings.

Not only did the early New England colonist face a new geographical environment and potentially hostile native inhabitants, but the extremely difficult job of providing for himself the necessities of life from a relatively poor soil was almost overwhelming. The challenges of the new environment were so great that the English settler almost disappeared because of starvation, privation, and Indian attacks long before he had time to establish himself with anything resembling permanency.

To meet these challenges, the Puritan lived under very strict controls of the land and of the economic system. The later reverence for the Puritan moral, economic, and political systems is somewhat exaggerated. The Puritans did not allow unfettered use of the land as later laissez faire proponents would have us believe. Neither did they establish a democratic system with political freedom and responsibility for all as later writers have claimed. In truth, early New England had a very rigid system dictated in part by natural conditions and by the experience in England. Land usage, in particular, was very carefully controlled. Man was a steward for the natural resources as the Bible taught, but he had also to control their use in order to maintain certain class standards and to promote the general welfare.

In early American history one of the overriding features was the almost unlimited amount of available land. Contrary to popular misconception, land was never free in America before the Homestead Act of 1862, but this does not deny the existence of overwhelming amounts of land, most of which could be acquired for a relatively low price. The availability of the land was the key feaure. Even if it were not free, and its acquisition may have been difficult, its availability had an impact on the European of undeterminable proportions. Land was here, and it was available to those with the ability and the luck to acquire it.

To the European, not far removed from feudalism, this was an almost unbelievable phenomenon. In Europe the land had been preempted for generations. The possibility for an average person from such an environment to own his own land was virtually nonexistent. Yet to the person from a feudal or semifeudal background where land was the one thing of permanence, it was mind-boggling to contemplate the unlimited amount of extremely fertile land available in North America. To conservative rural people the possibility of becoming landowners in the New World was such an exhilarating experience that they were willing to uproot themselves from the familiar surroundings in Europe for the dangerous and unpredictable journey to a new land.

To the European the attraction was not only that the land was here, but that as far as he was concerned it was uninhabited. No matter that the native Indian population viewed with suspicion the white man's coming and his methods of utilizing nature. To the European the Indian utilized only a very small portion of the territory and resources of this area. The American colonists very seldom considered the possibility that, within the Indian's social and economic systems, the land was fully utilized. Excessive population would (and subsequently history proved it true) destroy the natural habitat of wildlife and would, if continued long enough, destroy the

natural attractions of this region. The colonist could see only
that the land was virtually uninhabited and that it was not
utilized to its potential.

Almost from the beginning, therefore, we can see the
differences in attitudes toward nature. Nature provided the
Indian with all his needs. All he had to do was to live in
harmony with nature—maintain a low population, take only
what he immediately needed, and protect the natural wonders
—for his needs to be fulfilled forever. In essence, he was a
part of nature; moreover, he recognized and accepted this
status. The American colonist, however, saw the natural
wonders as something separate from himself—something
to be exploited and used, certainly never thinking about the
ultimate disastrous consequences.

The question of the proper utilization of the land and
resources appears throughout American history. A major
justification for moving against the Indians in every part of
the country was that the natural economic potential was not
exploited and realized. Since the Indian was a "primitive"
and needed less, he could be moved into the less desirable and
less productive land where, if it became necessary, he could
be cared for by government agents. Most of all, he should not
be allowed to stand in the way of progress. The vast reaches
of land could not be reserved for hunting; that land should
be put to the plow to produce unlimited staples.

Not only did the American consider the Indian culture
an economic obstacle; he was never particularly concerned
with the impact of his policy on the Indians themselves. Seldom did the American realize (or care) that the forcible or
negotiated movement of a tribe of Indians westward into new
territory created as many or more problems as it solved.
Indian cultures already existing in the West were no more
anxious to see other Indians moved in than they would wel-
come the white man. The forced movement of eastern Indians
westward encroached on the hunting grounds and the social
systems of those already in residence. In effect, such forced
migrations upset the ecological balance of the new region and

brought conflict among Indians as well as between Indians and whites.

Some historians contend that our treatment of the Indians was not necessarily motivated by economic considerations, but was, in truth, simply a manifestation of American racism. To support this argument, they use the well-known case of the Cherokees in Georgia.

One of the so-called Five Civilized Tribes, the Cherokees in Georgia decided that the white advance could not be stopped. Rather than follow a suicidal policy of resistance, they decided to adopt much of the life style of the whites themselves. In adapting to white culture, the Cherokees became landowners, farmers, and even in some instances owners of black slaves. From all outward appearances they were Southern planters with a different background. However, in the early nineteenth century the land held by the Indians became so valuable that the state of Georgia moved to evict the Cherokees from their homes. Since they had adopted white man's ways, the Cherokees decided to fight the action through legal procedures rather than to resist physically. On two occasions the Supreme Court under the leadership of Chief Justice John Marshall upheld the Indian claims. In the final analysis, however, the state of Georgia prevailed. In direct conflict with the Supreme Court, and with the tacit approval of President Andrew Jackson, the Indians were driven from their homes and marched overland in the dead of winter to a new land set aside for them in Indian Territory (Oklahoma). Known as the "trail of tears," this was one of the most terrible episodes in our history. Some 25 percent of the Indians died on the march; in addition, they were not welcomed by other Indians already in Oklahoma. President Jackson allowed this to happen partly because of his political rivalry with Chief Justice Marshall and partly because of his hatred of Indians intensified by his years as an Indian fighter before becoming President.

The critics of this episode contend that the Cherokees were moved not because of their economic system but because they were Indians. In truth, they argue, the Indians had be-

come capitalists of the American variety who were fully utilizing the land. Probably the motivation for this action was a
combination of economic rivalry and racism. The Cherokees
were successful planters who were in direct competition with
white Southerners. Such an economic challenge could have
been tolerated from others of the same ethnic heritage. However, to face competition from a "primitive" or "savage"
group was asking too much. Likewise, the land occupied by the
Indians was too valuable to be left in the control of what the
Georgian considered as an "alien" group.

The American, as he moved westward across the continent, objected to the use of nature by almost every group he
encountered. Among those who were most resented were the
Spanish and later the Mexicans who controlled the Southwest.
They were more advanced and should know how to use the
land better, he concluded. In the 1830s and 1840s, as the pressure for westward expansion intensified, the Southwest—at
first Spanish and then Mexican after 1821—was seen as an
area ripe for American expansion. The inability or the unwillingness of the Mexican government to exploit the area seemed
justification enough for a more progressive people—the Americans—to obtain it. It seemed inconceivable that such a potentially valuable area should be left undeveloped when a vigorous
and dynamic people waited eagerly to move into it. National
boundaries should not be allowed to stand in the way of
progress. America should offer to buy it, but if that failed, it
could be taken by force, as it eventually was in the Mexican
War.

It must be noted that American expansion in the pre–
Civil War period did not occur only at the expense of "primitive" or "backward" people. The British also came in for the
same treatment for essentially the same reasons. The Oregon
country was one of the most inviting and attractive areas in
the West. American interests and claims there dated from the
eighteenth century, but so did those of the British. For a number of years in the 1830s and 1840s, joint control and occupa-
tion was maintained over the area. It was not long, however,

before the British became alarmed that the growing American migration to the area would bring an end to the valuable fur trade. The maintenance of an abundant supply of fur-bearing animals depended very largely on keeping the area as thinly settled as possible. It was this emphasis on small settlement that brought American demands for total control of the area. The unlimited potential of the Oregon country was not realized and never would be if the British had their way. In the final analysis, the Oregon country was acquired by the United States through a compromise that approximately halved the area in dispute. Although many Americans were disappointed that not all of it was obtained, half seemed better than nothing. This episode helped to convince many Americans that the British were no more advanced than the Indians or Mexicans, because they could not see the potential of the area for exploitation.

This emphasis on westward expansion was termed, at the time, "manifest destiny." One might argue that a discussion of manifest destiny might more appropriately be included when discussing attitudes or government policy. Although this may be true, manifest destiny is also a reflection of the American economic system. The acquisition of territory was basic to the growth concepts of capitalism.

There seem to be two answers to the question of why the American was not willing to limit his expansionist urge and develop the land he already had more fully before moving on to new areas. First, as already emphasized, the lure of the land was there. The prospect of its going unused, or underused, was just too much to accept. Second, the accumulation of land and the speculation on its value were already a part of what was the American version of capitalism. The profit potential from skyrocketing land prices was so great that we had, to a great extent, already become a nation of real estate brokers. When one looks at the broad sweep of westward expansion, he is often struck by the realization that expansion, and, to a large degree, all American economic development, were based on speculation. From the beginning right down to the present time, few purchasers of land or property intended to stay on it permanently. It was purchased on the assumption that its value would appreciate rapidly, and it could be sold at a good, sometimes enormous, profit. Thus, long-range planning was seldom a part of the individual's motivation when acquiring property.

In the late nineteenth century there was a rebirth of the spirit that prevailed before the Civil War. Known as the "new manifest destiny," it was even more a manifestation or reflection of American capitalism. By that time the basic and developmental phase of the Industrial Revolution was reaching its peak. American businessmen were rapidly learning a very important lesson about mass production—industrialized and urbanized nations must have a large and dependable source of raw materials and a steadily increasing market. To put it very bluntly, American industrial capacity had already outdistanced the public's ability to consume. The United States, obviously, was not the only nation to discover this phenomenon—most western European nations as well as Japan had already begun the acquisition of colonial empires in the underdeveloped world in order to augment and support their industrial capacities.

American interest in the new manifest destiny did not necessarily mean that we were destined to become a colonial power. We could exert influence in ways other than direct political control to maintain safe and reliable sources of raw materials and markets. The advocacy of "open door" policies or the practice of "dollar diplomacy" had their limitations, however. Too often it was relatively simple for plans to be thwarted by international rivals or by local residents who resented outside interference. Many Americans, like industrial nations worldwide, eventually concluded that the best way to protect sources and markets was to own them outright. The need for international expansion coincided conveniently with the rise of social Darwinism and determinism which helped to justify such overseas expansion. Thus, we did acquire the Philippines, Hawaii, Puerto Rico, the Canal Zone, and virtual ownership of Cuba. Some have contended that the United

States was never a colonial power in the same way that Britain or France were, but the question seems academic. The differences seem to be more a matter of form than anything else. The crucial matter was that if the American economic system were to remain dynamic, vital, and evergrowing, markets and sources of raw material had to be maintained one way or another. Without constant and steady penetration into new areas, the American economic system would slow down, become static, and eventually decline.

One question, ignored so far, is of great importance. How does such expansionism with its relationship to the economic system influence or affect the environment? The answer lies in an examination of the utilization of the land and of the resources it provided.

To put it simply, Americans have from the very beginning exploited nature unmercifully. Such a statement seems inconsistent, however, when compared with the traditional view of the American character in an earlier era. Social and intellectual historians have pointed out that Americans were, until the very recent past, at least, a poor people. By necessity, the early pioneer and farmer were frugal and thrifty. Many stories are told of how nothing was wasted, of how farms were as self-sufficient as possible, and of how the pioneer farmer was the first conservationist. Such characterizations seem to be true, but they do not tell the whole story. Americans were thrifty with money and other things in short supply. With resources which they had in great abundance, they did not prove to be so cautious.

Professor Leo E. Oliva[1] has explained very well how little concern for the environment there was among our pioneer forebears. He explains how the various waves of settlement— the trapper, miner, rancher, farmer—moved in, took what they could of the surface wealth, and moved out, leaving the remnants to those who followed. This is probably best exemplified by the story he relates from Polk County, Missouri. "In those old days farmers used to brag about how many farms they had worn out. Those old boys used to say, 'Why son, by the time I was your age I had wore out three farms.' "[2] In addition, he quotes from several foreign observers who were appalled by the American's attitude toward nature. The foreign visitors were especially struck by the American's dislike of trees. As Professor Oliva says, "Because forests were hard to clear and harbored Indians, they were considered obstacles to settlement and development. A lingering dislike, perhaps hatred, of trees survived the initial confrontation."[3] In regard to clearing land, one foreign observer noted that "felling, burning, rooting up, tearing down, lopping, and chopping, are all employed with the most unrelenting severity."[4] Another foreign visitor noted that Americans had no conception of the beauty and majesty of trees. In describing the American, he said, "To him a country well cleared, that is where every stick is cut down, seems the only one that is beautiful or worthy of admiration."[5]

Trees were not, of course, the only resources that came under attack. In some ways they were only the most visible symbols of nature. All forms of natural beauty and wealth were relentlessly exploited until, in many cases, they were virtually destroyed. In sum, the American, with notable exceptions, was prodigal with the things of nature.

Looking back, we can say that the advantages produced by these practices could have been achieved with greater efficiency and with protection of the environment by simply moving a little slower and working with nature instead of against her. We can look back smugly and say that our grandfathers should have known better—that confronted with the same situation today we would deal with it more effectively.

Before self-righteousness overwhelms us, we should look at the current record. What motivates a housing developer to buy a farm, clear it of all growth, build subdivisions, and then sell the lots and houses with the promise and inducement that a large number of trees have been planted? What motivates the Missouri farmer to spray poison on trees with crop dusting planes so that grass will grow between the dead trees and he can raise more cattle? The long-range impact of poisons, pesti-

cides, flooding, erosion, and wildlife is serious enough, but
when one considers that trees are producers of oxygen, a basic
part of the life cycle for humans, the overwhelming long-range
influence of such actions (against their short-run benefits)
becomes more obvious. Strip-mining and channelization of
streams for irrigation and navigation purposes are two other
similar activities with unrealized potential for long-range
damage.

What all this means is simply this: from Jamestown to the
present time we have utilized those things of nature which
benefit us in the short run with little concern for the long-
range consequences. When something loses its value or use-
fulness, we readily discard it with little concern. One only has
to drive through parts of rural America to see discarded automobiles, broken or obsolete farm equipment, and junk of all
kinds. Urban slums with their waste are a familiar sight to
most of us. Obviously, this is not anything new. Early records
tell us that colonial America was confronted with garbage and
filth in the cities and litter in the country. Cynics have mar-
veled at the magnificent job of restoration made with Rocke-
feller Foundation money at colonial Williamsburg. The community has been very accurately restored down to the last
detail, with one exception—the dirt and filth of the community have not been restored nor have the hogs that originally
roamed the streets as scavengers nor the garbage collectors
been returned to complete the picture. Obviously, such eye-
sores would have little attraction for today's tourist, but, unfortunately, many of the historic sites maintained by various
agencies leave the impression that our forebears were paragons
of neatness and cleanliness. A bit of delving into the records
soon dispels such a notion.

Today's problems of pollution are, to a large extent, a
continuation of habits ingrained early in the American experience. One has only to look at the mounting garbage problems
and the massive landfills to see how we consider nature. One
of the startling facts comes when we realize that we have
begun the same practice in a virgin area—space. Remember

all the expensive junk we have left on the moon and all the satellites, launchers, and other debris that have been discarded in space. Unfortunately, some historians of the future may record that one of America's unique characteristics was the building of junkyards from Jamestown to the moon—and beyond.

It may seem that we have drifted far afield in the original discussion of capitalism. Yet, when we consider why many of these problems have developed, one of the obvious villains in the piece is capitalism with its overriding profit motive. Why, for example, has all the expensive equipment been abandoned on the moon and dumped in space? One reason may be that technology is developed only to the point where space ships and crews can be returned to the earth safely. It just might also be due to the fact that the cost of returning such equipment is prohibitive. The environmentalist might contend, in such instances, that space probes not be made until technology is capable of returning everything to earth that it sends out of the atmosphere. Is that asking too much?

One other example of the pervasiveness of the profit motive will suffice. In various parts of the country, local efforts to promote the recycling of reusable materials have been promoted with mixed results. In some cases the projects have been quite successful, but in many the programs have faced many difficulties, including the public relations problem of convincing the public that recycling is a worthy cause. More important, however, is that the programs are often economically hard to justify. To make a profit from recycling materials is very difficult. The point of recycling, we are told, is to put to use those things that people discard; but when considerations of profit enter the picture, the original goal is often obscured. Yet, if recycling is designed to save precious mineral supplies by reusing certain materials, should not recycling be required by law even if it increases costs to the consumer? It is at this point that the degree of one's commitment to environmental protection becomes clear.

Despite the attitudes prevalent before the Civil War, the

American capitalist system did not really offer a serious threat to the environment until the Industrial Revolution was in full swing in the late nineteenth century. Two things in particular combined to endanger the ecosystem more seriously than ever before—population and mass production. These two forces are mutually dependent upon one another, and they go hand in hand. The industrial process has an almost insatiable appetite for the products of nature. Mass production requires that such materials be so readily available on such a scale that the proper and orderly acquisition of nature's bounties is not possible. Industrialization also requires a larger and larger population to produce the goods that require a larger population to consume them.

Despite all the controversy surrounding it, one cannot deny that the process of American industrialization was one of the wonders of the modern world. In less than half a century, the United States was transformed from a rural, agrarian nation to one of the world's greatest industrial producers. By American standards at the time, this was progress in its most meaningful definition. The material benefits were overwhelming. The living standard eventually became the highest in the world; even those Americans at or below the defined poverty line had a much higher standard of living than many millions of people around the world. It made possible the support of a population undreamed of only a century or so ago. It has given the world gadgets and machines beyond our wildest expectations. It resulted in the greatest and most efficient productive capacity ever known to man.

In the face of such an assessment, the defenders of industrialization are mystified today when environmentalists are critical of the system. The latter appear to be reformers bent only on change for its own sake. If capitalism and American know-how have made all this possible, why, the defenders ask, do these do-gooders or troublemakers want to tamper with it? If the system is tampered with too much, the argument runs, it will be destroyed and all mankind will suffer. Such discussion has become much more animated with the recent discovery of an energy crisis. Reformers should be content with its benefits and leave well enough alone. The alternative is to condemn all Americans to a much more bleak existence, or as one prominent leader said recently, "Pollution smells better than poverty." In addition, the chairman of Bethlehem Steel entered the debate. Reacting to a poll that showed that 46 percent of the public thinks that big business is "dangerous to our way of life," he answered with several rhetorical questions. "Would nearly every American family have a car if it weren't for so-called big business? Would we have telephones and television and indoor plumbing in most homes? Would we have the levels of education and nutrition and health care that, however imperfect, are the envy of almost everyone else on this planet?"[6] His reaction to criticism was a kind of "know-nothingism" or anti-intellectualism reminiscent of an earlier day. His attitude seems to be about as realistic as that of the Luddite rioters in England who thought they could eliminate automation and resulting unemployment during the early days of the Industrial Revolution by smashing the machines which they believed to be the source of their troubles.

With an attitude almost as narrow-minded, our modern corporate leaders never seem to realize that the question of the social benefits of automobiles and television sets are the real questions that critics of American technology are raising today: whether the bounties provided by industrialization and technology are worth the astronomically high economic, social, and natural costs. They are asking whether it is truly desirable for every American family to have an automobile and a television set. Perhaps, they conclude, we cannot, as only one nation on spaceship Earth, afford such luxuries.

When one examines the historical record of industrial growth, he may conclude that the critics are correct. Within a very limited time span, we denuded our hillsides of virgin forests; we gutted the earth of a mineral treasure unequaled for quality and diversity anywhere else in the world; and we contaminated crystal-clear rivers and streams even to the point that some of them have become fire hazards. Only in recent years have we become somewhat aware of the immensity of the physical change we have wrought on the countryside. We are forced to face the realization that such reckless utilization of resources may well have provided for our posterity a weakened and desolate country that may not even be able to provide the necessities of life, not to mention the luxuries of cars and television. Perhaps a more rational utilization of resources would have made possible the same growth, albeit on a small scale over a longer time period, and provided more of the same development for a longer time in the future.

Often such questions are dismissed as purely academic, given the nature of our economic system. Capitalism, as defined in America, is an exploitative, profit-oriented system that seldom allows for rational use of resources and for rational growth. Because of its extreme competitive nature, the entrepreneur who worried about the purity of water or air or who concerned himself about protecting trees was left behind in the economic race. The captains of industry, some claim, would have been only lieutenants or sergeants had they been concerned about the social and historical results of their actions. One had to grasp the opportunities when they were available or be left behind. After all, "He who hesitates is lost." Some also rationalized their irresponsible actions on the assumption that someone else would have done it if they had not. Obviously, such a system seldom considered the actual need for an industry or whether it was socially desirable.

One of the best examples of the irrationality of the system involved the building of the transcontinental railroads and the so-called robber-baron thesis. The idea of a rail link between California and the settled part of the country east of the Mississippi River had excited the country as soon as railroads became a reality before the Civil War. Construction was not possible before the Civil War, however, because sectional differences prevented a political decision on the proper route. As soon as the Southern states seceded and withdrew their representatives from Congress, action was taken to authorize and subsidize a transcontinental railroad.

At that point few people questioned if such a system was socially desirable. Unfortunately, however, the irresponsible way in which the first transcontinental railroad was built set a pattern of waste and corruption that caused difficulties far into the future. To speed up construction, Congress authorized two companies, starting at opposite terminal points and working toward one another, to build the line as rapidly as possible. Each line's government subsidy was based on the number of miles of track constructed. The result is well known. The race to lay as many miles of track as possible resulted in such shoddy construction that the road had to be almost totally rebuilt within a decade. The impact of the railroad on the environment, wildlife (especially the buffalo), and Indian inhabitants was hardly considered.

Later other lines were built, with and without federal aid, until four major transcontinental systems were completed. One could ask if four such lines were needed, particularly when two of them were in direct competition. The question, again, is academic. The railroad caught the imagination of Americans, and we encouraged its massive and rapid construction. Need was little considered. The railroad was a quick way for enterprising and daring entrepreneurs to make a profit, and it was all in the true spirit of American competition. The creation of the so-called robber baron came as a direct result of the railroad boom. As time passed, the uncomplimentary name was attached to all businessmen who were considered unscrupulous in their dealings with the public. Undoubtedly, many were of this type, but many others who were honest but ruthless were unfairly given the name by their opponents.

Actually, persons of this type were acting in the way that the American system made possible. Without planning and political or economic restraints, they were able to take advantage of the public and to exploit its resources without ever committing acts that were technically illegal. For a long time the public generally approved of their actions since they were only capitalists who took advantage of the opportunities presented to them. Even after investigations proved the dishonesty

of many of the promoters, both large and small, a large seg-
ment of the public still condoned their actions. They may have
been unscrupulous and possibly unethical, the argument stated,
but the job had to be done; they should not be blamed just because they were successful. Furthermore, the railroads were
needed, and the final result was worth the cost. Even if the
public were looted of great wealth, the result was the construction of a much-needed, vast railroad network.

Obviously, at the time of the building of the railroads,
virtually no one raised the question of how the construction
affected the environment. In truth, the problem was probably
not even recognized. As other giant industries developed in that
period and later, those who questioned the environmental benefit received no hearing at all. In fact, it was not until the
twentieth century that even the faint voices of conservationists
protested the despoliation of nature. But since the problem had
not become generally apparent by that time, they were usually
ignored.

One of the aspects of this period not often considered in
this context was the social cost of the Industrial Revolution.
Not only did the American brand of capitalism exploit the natural resources, but it also exploited and transformed our human
resources. One feature that most people did not recognize until
it had already developed was the awesome power that the
great wealth of the captains of industry bestowed.

In the late nineteenth century a relatively small group of
business and financial leaders acquired so much wealth that
they virtually controlled the entire lives of those associated
with them. Even if many dismissed this group as a crude,
gaudy example of the nouveau riche, it did not diminish the
fact that their wealth gave them greater power over the lives
of individuals, if one disregards American slavery, than at any
time since the Middle Ages. The use of the term "robber
baron" by their critics was not accidental. This was a deliberate
attempt to compare the giants of American industry to the
medieval barons of Europe. The analogy was drawn very
tightly. The industrialist was the same as the baron who owned

the manor and all the land surrounding it. The worker was the modern serf who was tied to the baron economically and could not leave the manor (factory) without the risk of serious consequences. The medieval knight was the baron's retainer whose duty was to protect the baron and his possessions from outside dangers. In the modern context, critics claimed, the knights were the various levels of management and the private police whose primary duties were to keep the serfs (workers) peaceful and under control by acting as spies and union breakers. The major difference between the baron and the industrialist was that the baron had the well-being of his serfs and the general public in mind, whereas the modern industrialist could not care less about the worker or the general public. He had become, they contended, really a *robber* baron. Originally applying to only the railroad promoters as already mentioned, the term came eventually to apply to most business leaders as far as much of the public was concerned. People like Mark Twain could satirize the period, as he did in his famous book *The Gilded Age,* but scoffing and ridicule did not change the actual situation.

The power of such giants of industry and finance did not apply only to economic matters; the power extended to matters of public policy as well. When men like Cornelius Vanderbilt, Jay Gould, and Jim Fiske could virtually buy a state legislature as they did in New York in their fight to control the Erie Railroad, something obviously had gone wrong with Jefferson's dream of an America composed of sturdy yeoman farmers. When Gould and Fiske could corner the gold market in 1869, albeit with the unwitting aid of President Grant, there were those who questioned where the power in America resided. But perhaps the most obvious and frightening manifestation of power came in 1894. In that depression year the government's gold supply was in serious danger of being depleted. When President Cleveland was eventually forced to go privately to J. P. Morgan, the financier, to ask him to use his influence to raise a foreign loan, it was inevitable for some to ask who really ran the government. The question was not really academic; it forced the realization of an uncomfortable fact that most people would have been just as happy to ignore.

Very much related to the Industrial Revolution and the power of the industrial elite was the urban blight just becoming apparent in the late nineteenth century. Jefferson's fear that the city would become a blot upon civilization was, in fact, coming true. But it did not have to be that way. With proper planning and control, the city could have remained a pleasant place to live while, at the same time, providing a home for industry, finance, communication, and trade.

The causes of undesirable urban growth are many. Urban historians are presently examining city growth with the goal of discovering what went wrong and possibly finding a way to correct it now and to avoid its intensification and recurrence in the future. Despite the absence of definite proof, we can at least point to a few things that contributed to urban problems.

To a certain extent, the deterioration of the city was the result of the traditional urban-rural antagonism in the United States. The fear and distrust between these two elements has been defined. Rural dwellers have always felt themselves to be the holders of the best way of life possible. Farming was not just a way of making a living; it was, in truth, a "way of life." Jefferson's idealization of this had merely supported a widely-held view that Richard Hofstadter called "the agrarian myth."[7] Rural people had felt the lure and pull of the city from the beginning, but the older and more traditional defenders of agrarianism retained the hope and belief that the younger generation attracted to the city would eventually recognize and admit their wrong choice and return to the soil. As far as these defenders were concerned, the city was a totally evil and demoralizing place.

Conversely, the urban dweller looked upon his country cousin as a bumpkin, a hayseed, a hick. He was the hillbilly come to the city to be hoodwinked by the slicker. With such an attitude, it is no wonder that the Brooklyn Bridge was sold over and over again. The snobbery involved in this attitude

can be seen in such contemporary attitudes as the absolute belief of many that nothing of value existed west of the Hudson
River.

With such varied attitudes, cooperation and planning were
most difficult to achieve. Rurally controlled legislatures were
not anxious to spend money on cities; the country feared the
potential power of the urban center; many city residents were
fresh from the farm and did not consider themselves a permanent part of the urban landscape. As a result, urban development was mostly ignored.

Despite contributing causes such as these, the overriding
influence, however, on urban growth was the American economic system. American cities, for the most part, came into
existence and grew as a part of the Industrial Revolution.
Their primary function was to serve American industry. The
establishment of a factory caused workers to move nearby because transportation was not developed sufficiently to allow
them to commute from relatively long distances. Available
labor and transportation—usually rail or water—facilities
caused other industries to move into an already settled area.
The new industry, in turn, attracted more workers who attracted service businesses to meet their needs. Thus, almost
before anyone realized it, urban sprawl, with little or no controls in the form of zoning or other regulations, had begun.

Business needed cities; cities were built by and for the
benefit of business. Yet businessmen were reluctant to take
responsibility for the type of city that developed. It is little
wonder that life in the city deteriorated rapidly, and as soon
as it was logistically possible, the movement to the suburbs—
creating new and unique urban problems—began.

One other side effect of the economic system and the
power of industry was the exploitation and humiliation of the
worker in the system. Labor, originally highly skilled and re-
spected, now found itself simply one part of the production
process. Management sought labor at its lowest cost and thus
contributed to some of our most serious social problems. Immigration was encouraged with the belief that a continuing

supply of labor contributed to industrial growth by keeping wages low. Little consideration was given to the resulting social friction, urban slums, and pressures on social agencies. Labor organization was resisted so strongly that strikes and violence became a part of the industrial scene. The worker in this new situation found himself forced to live in an undesirable city, to compete with foreigners whom he considered beneath him, and to be at the mercy of the business cycle which often denied him even demeaning work. Obviously, his new place in society was much below that of an earlier time.

One might argue that social problems created by the Industrial Revolution should not be included in a discussion of the ecological crisis of today. It seems clear, however, that we must recognize that an ecosystem is a total system. We must also consider the past and the future of the human factor in the delicate ecological balance. Then, we must also recognize that the cause of human and social problems is the same as for the destruction of the natural environment. American capitalism is very much one of the villains. A virtually uncontrolled capitalistic economy is exploitative of everything in its path and is concerned about only one thing—profit, the reason for its existence. In sum, industrial growth has been narrow-minded with little or no consideration of its side effects, whether natural or human.

Again, this is not an attack upon the "American way of life" by a demogogue or an ideologist. What is suggested is this: at this particular point in time we must examine our economic system with a realistic view about what it is and what it is not. Foremost, the system must be humanized and made to have a social consciousness. Great progress has been made in this direction since the nineteenth century. More and more firms have realized that they not only produce goods, but that they also contribute to the social atmosphere and bear a large degree of responsibility for the product they produce. The humanization process is not complete, however; it needs, in fact, to be speeded up.

More than this, the American people must examine the

system dispassionately; they must decide what is good and bad about it. They must decide if the concept of an ever-growing gross national product is desirable. If not, some way must be devised to continue to benefit from the wonders of industry and technology without destroying ourselves in the process.

Such a self-examination will be the most difficult thing we have to do. Unfortunately, too many people have equated capitalism with democracy; a critique of one thus becomes a critique of the other. Some way must be devised to disabuse the public of such a view. We must recognize that economic and political systems have distinct functions. If the American people decide to modify capitalism or to discard it altogether, there is nothing inherently wrong with this decision as long as it is made by the traditional democratic process.

Without doubt, a solution of the ecological crisis will necessitate an economic revolution. There will be those who do not like the changes, and there will be those who think they are long overdue. Above all, we must recognize the fact that the system must be scrutinized as dispassionately as possible. It is a large order for Americans, but it must be done.

5

THE POLITICAL REVOLUTION

In any discussion of the environmental crisis, the question inevitably arises as to what can be done about it and who can do it. In casual conversation or serious planning, various suggestions are made about voluntary cooperation between business and industry or self-regulation by the groups that most seriously foul the environment. The discussion eventually leads to exploratory talks about state or local regulation and control. If the discussion continues long enough, the role of the federal government eventually emerges.

At that point the real issue has been joined. To bring about changes of any sort requires the availability of and the willingness to use power. Power is the key. Discussion can continue ad infinitum about cooperation and self-regulation, but it is only when the sources of power and the means to exercise it are sought that the problem really comes into perspective.

One may proclaim the virtues of state and local control and power as much as he wishes, but modern history teaches us several things—the most basic of which is that power tends to gravitate toward the center and to cluster around a central figure or body. American history bears this out. A study of our past shows that there has been a steady flow of power from the rural areas and local groups to the states, and eventually to the federal government. A second lesson is that local government has no innate ability to be good, honest, efficient, or fair. Events of the past and present reveal that some of the greatest inefficiency and the most gross corruption occur on the local level. Admittedly, the centralized level has much the same problem. One seems as good (or bad) as the other. Third, problems as massive as environmental control not only transcend local boundaries but are worldwide in scope. Therefore, probably the smallest area in which they can be dealt with, given the nature and extent of nationalism today, is the national area.

If the environmentalist is agreed that most action must eventually come from the federal government, several things must be determined and understood. First, one must know what the federal government is and what it is not. Second, he must learn where the power actually resides at the federal level. Third, he must assess what the government's attitude toward the environment has been in the past and what it is today. And finally, he must devise some method by which he can turn that power toward his ultimate objective—the salvation of the environment. The answers to these questions are not easy to find. However, if such control of the federal government were to be achieved, it would constitute little less than a political revolution.

Throughout most of our history the federal government has been personified by a few outstanding political leaders. Americans have always, with a few exceptions, looked to presidents or others at the national level as repositories of national power, but very seldom has this been a true picture of the government. Individual leaders may have their followings in government and among the public, but unless they are also near the hidden sources of power, they are able to effect little change. For example, "peoples' " movements have never been able to make much headway unless they were supported by the often silent and unseen persons who can make things happen. These movements usually make a lot of noise, offer many promises, and then go down in defeat.

Actually, the federal government is almost never a molder of public opinion nor a leader in bringing new ideas before the public. It is basically a sluggish, slow-moving apparatus that accepts public attitudes that have already been current for some time. The public generally approves of this and does not desire a forward-looking, experimental government. Probably one of the major reasons why the Supreme Court has been so controversial since 1954 is that its decisions are far ahead of the thinking of the mass of the public. The changes it makes are far-reaching and advanced. The government has been as much a follower as it has been a leader or maker of opinion. There have existed occasionally those lonely and often ostracized and frustrated political leaders who promote an unpopular cause before its time has arrived. They usually wage lonely and politically dangerous campaigns with little success. Later, when the government catches up with public opinion, these people are acclaimed as pioneers before their time even though some of them do not live to see their goals reached. The truth of the matter is that the American government, whether called liberal or conservative, is not very adventuresome.

One of the most important, though not necessarily apparent, repositories of power in the national government is the massive bureaucracy. This is neither indictment nor praise; it is a simple statement of fact. The flashy, personable individuals who hold public office often overshadow the bureaucrat and appear to be the movers and shakers of public policy; but much of the real power to make the government function lies within the various agencies, departments, and bureaus where the day-to-day working decisions are made. Bureaucrats are basically unknown or invisible people who are little recognized by the general public for what they are. They most often remain a faceless mass until they become obstacles in the way of achieving some goal. Then, according to some studies, the bureaucrat gets gleeful pleasure from exerting his power and making the uncaring public uncomfortable. Other studies have shown that they have little contact, or perhaps even interest, in the world outside the government, even though they exert enormous amounts of power. Parkinson[1] was exactly correct when he stated that bureaucracies tend to perpetuate themselves. He used as an example the Admiralty and Colonial Office of the British government, which increased its staff by 5 to 6 percent each year even though the naval and colonial activities of the government were decreasing. Bureaucracies have to justify their existence and prove a need for expansion. This is done by taking on or assuming more functions and responsibilities even if the need does not exist, as it did not in the British Empire.

In addition to its size, the bureaucracy is usually responsible for the success or failure of government programs. Although the elected public official may take daring positions and commit himself, and tacitly the government, to a program, such action often is totally meaningless. The actual achievement of goals is in the hands of sometimes minor or petty bureaucrats; their degree of commitment to and belief in a program will usually determine its success. Unless the public is really aroused and demands action (a rare occurrence), rapid or significant changes are most unlikely; even then bureaucrats are often impervious to such stimulation. A major part of the political revolution is to educate ourselves to the ways of bureaucracy and to find a way of mobilizing it into action for the protection of the environment.

Other major sources of power at the federal level are the various interest groups whose primary purpose is to influence legislation and government action for their own benefit. Despite laws requiring the identification of lobbyists, there are innumerable ones who are totally unknown to the general public. Because of the lack of information, attitudes about them are often quite inflated. Various studies have revealed some degree of the massive power they have.[2] For the environmentalist, the challenge with this group is not to motivate it to constructive environmental action, but somehow to blunt its power and effectiveness in obtaining government action that allows for environmental destruction. Occasionally, inter-

est groups may become concerned about environmental spoliation, but they will more likely be interested in exploitation.

The other facet, of course, is to discover what environmental policy the government has followed in the past. If its
public stance does not seem satisfactory, then action is necessary to see that the position changes. The real issue here is
to force the government to respond to the needs of today and
tomorrow. Any government that ceases to be responsive to
general attitudes and concerns eventually loses its base of support and its reason for existence. If the environmentalist concludes that the government has not done its part in protecting
the environment, then it must be persuaded, pressured, or
forced into recognizing the need and into taking appropriate
action. There is no reason to assume that the form of government should be changed; that would be necessary only if it
proved totally unresponsive to current needs.

What specifically has been the government's historical attitude toward the environment? The answer is not so simple.
Basically, the government has had no environmental position
because, until very recently, there seemed little need. No
danger to the environment was observed by any more than a
small fraction of the public. Moreover, the powerful interests,
from landowners and miners to industrialists, were quite concerned that no policy of hindrance should be adopted. Therefore, the government drifted along, responding only when
there was a crisis, either natural or political, and occasionally
enacting rather innocuous legislation ostensibly designed for
conservation. Only recently has the government begun to feel
the shock waves of the current ecological concern and to respond somewhat haphazardly to the new pressures. But before dealing with the current situation, a closer look at the
historical record is necessary.

From the very beginning of English settlement in North
America, the government, whether British or American, has
cooperated with those who have exploited the environment.
Admittedly, when faced with the seemingly unlimited wealth
and expanse of the continent, virtually no one gave any

thought to possible dangers to the natural habitat. In fact, it is probably correct to say that at the beginning, there *was* no danger. The question under consideration here is what the attitude of the government was and what was its impact on nature, either conscious or unconscious.

The government cooperated fully from the beginning because the prevailing economic system, mercantilism, emphasized a direct cooperation between government and business. Government aided and cooperated with business interests for its own benefit; a commercial enterprise had no legal basis for existence without the expressed grant of a charter from the government. The most profitable use—both economically and politically—of the resources of nature was the primary goal of the government. If this meant exploiting a specific natural resource because it would make the government richer and stronger in its rivalry with its neighbors, that was justification enough for its uncontrolled use.

After America won its independence from Great Britain, a new economic theory known as "laissez faire" was developed by Adam Smith.[3] According to Smith, there were certain natural laws that operated in the economic sphere of a nation's life. Smith was, of course, very much in tune with his own age—the eighteenth century—which has become known as the Enlightenment, or Age of Reason. Men were searching for the laws of nature that governed every part of the universe. Just as the movements of heavenly bodies were regular and in a pattern, or just as there were natural political rights as spelled out by John Locke and enacted by the American Revolution, Smith said there are natural laws that govern the buying and selling within human society. The most important of these laws, he said, was the law of supply and demand. If the marketplace is allowed to operate without outside or artificial interference, this law will balance the supply of goods to correspond with the demand. There will be times, for one reason or another, when an imbalance exists, but if left alone, the law will force the economic system to return to a normal flow of goods. Among the most important results of Smith's ideas was his impact on the role that government had previously played in economic matters.

The French term "laissez faire" implied that the government no longer had any role in the economic life of the nation. Competition and free trade were the new ideals. Unfettered by government involvement, every business would rise or fall on its own merits. This meant then, in its pure form, that laissez faire allowed each businessman to attempt to do virtually anything he wished. Businessmen were subject only to the various natural laws that affected every phase of life and the rules of human decency. If they were strong, they would grow and prosper by eliminating their competition; if they were weak, they would fail. It was truly the "survival of the fittest."

Laissez faire was not immediately adopted by any country. It appeared, on the surface, to be an antinationalistic policy that would weaken governments. Kings were suspicious of its potential threat. So for some time after Smith published his ideas in 1776, mercantilism continued to rule the day. Gradually, however, Smith's ideas could be seen infiltrating government policy; by the early nineteenth century laissez faire had become a respectable economic theory. No nation ever became totally laissez faire, but some of them approached that condition closely and many more proclaimed themselves to have achieved it.

The United States was one nation that called itself laissez faire even though that was not a totally accurate description. Laissez faire meant that the government should have no influence on the economy; it should neither hinder nor aid business activity. Most Americans fully embraced the first part of this concept. Business, they believed, should never be controlled or regulated by governmental power; such action would violate the law of supply and demand. American businessmen were never able, however, to embrace the entire laissez faire system. It was a rare businessman who refused government aid.

From the beginning of our national life, pressures were applied to encourage government support for business. Alexander Hamilton, for example, argued for a protective tariff, a direct violation of laissez faire, to defend America's "infant industries" from unfair foreign competition. Hamilton did not achieve his objective during his own lifetime. Not until after the War of 1812 when America was faced with enormous competition from English factories did Congress enact the first protective tariff bill, in 1816. From that date onward the tariff became one of the hottest political issues in American history. Interestingly, those groups opposed to protection rarely used the laissez faire argument in their fight against it; they more often rallied around regional economic differences and the impact of the tariff on different sections of the country. With the rise of industrial America, the Republican Party and its businessmen allies became the chief supporters of high tariffs long after the "infant" industries that Hamilton was concerned with became overgrown adolescents. The tariff was of obvious benefit to American businessmen, and they meant to keep it, even if it violated the laissez faire principles they so loudly proclaimed. One of their major activities through the nineteenth and twentieth centuries has been to convince Congress of the need for special favors for special industries.

Examples of other government aid to business are too numerous to mention. Government support ranges from the tariff to direct subsidies for many industries, to special tax benefits, to any number of other hidden favors. The scope of direct and indirect government aid to business is really stupendous, and it has most often been justified on the basis of national needs.

In addition to understanding the sources of power, anyone who hopes to change American political attitudes or policy must also be aware of the emotional objections he will encounter. Suggestions that change of a political nature is necessary often bring charges of disloyalty. Throughout the past Americans have usually been able to see political questions only in either-or terms—one is either for you or against you. Because this often leads to sloganeering rather than rational political discussion, progress in making meaningful change becomes very difficult.

The origin of such a state of mind is difficult to ascertain. Some historians have suggested that the conspiracy theory of history, the conviction that an organized plot exists to take control away from those who should rightfully hold it, is responsible for the suspicion toward suggestions for change from traditional methods. Critics have observed that a people susceptible to this view have an inflated opinion of themselves. Such people seem to think that they and their system are so superior that they are the envy of the rest of the world; everyone else wants what they have and is willing to go to any lengths to obtain it. Perhaps such an attitude is more likely to be accepted by a wealthy people or one with a special sense of mission.

That would, of course, fit in perfectly with American history. The United States has been richly blessed with almost unlimited resources that have been exploited and highly developed by an industrious people. Many Americans see the rest of the world as lazy and indigent, its people looking longingly toward America's wealth and waiting only for a sign of weakness or indecisiveness to take it away from them.

In addition, Americans have always thought of themselves as a people with a special mission. Puritan theology, with its emphasis on election and predestination, emphasized that Americans were a special chosen people on an "errand into the wilderness." Although they did not necessarily accept the specific Puritan theology, later Americans were quick to pick up and follow the concept. The emergence of the idea of manifest destiny in overseas expansion in the late nineteenth century was only a further refinement of this special-mission concept. Twentieth-century manifestations can be seen in the attitude that world wars were European-caused events that required superior American intervention to save Western civilization from the barbaric hordes, and in the American fear of communism as a threat to the safety and security of civilized people. Its destruction, or at least its reasonable containment, became a national policy of defense in the twentieth century.

A people so convinced of their special destiny and of the

existence of sinister forces at work to defeat their good works will often react in a hostile and even hysterical fashion in order to root out and destroy the threat. Periodically we have such outbursts. Probably the first such outburst was the trial of suspected witches in colonial Massachusetts. The Puritans believed that they had developed such a perfect society that the devil made special efforts to destroy it through the use of witches. The attempts to destroy the witch threat set a precedent for future outbursts of hysteria, including the antiforeign and anti-Catholic sentiment in the pre–Civil War period and again in the late nineteenth and early twentieth centuries. Anticommunist hysteria in the post–World War I period ("the red scare") and under the leadership of Joe McCarthy in the late 1940s and early 1950s are further examples. Extremist organizations, often right-wing groups such as the Ku Klux Klan and the John Birch Society, rely very heavily on the conspiracy theory to justify their actions. The use of patriotic rhetoric helps to make them more respectable.

Obviously, the American people react wildly to challenges to traditional means and to anything that suggests that our system is less than perfect. People who hold such concepts do not readily accept differing political views that question the basic assumptions about government. Just as a suggestion that internal or foreign threats are exaggerated would be rejected out-of-hand, so too, even though we are no longer a laissez faire nation, even in name, many people today would not be willing to admit it. The problem, to a very great extent, is that our political system does not adapt readily to changes that have already occurred. Therefore, any reformer is faced with a very serious challenge even before he gets to the real question of the environment.

Beginning with mercantilism, the United States moved gradually into a modified laissez faire position in the nineteenth century and then into welfare-state capitalism in the twentieth century. Unfortunately, with each change numerous individuals and groups have denied or refused to admit that such changes have, in fact, occurred. Obviously, if one is faced with such unwillingness to face reality, a realistic change in government attitudes toward the environment will be most difficult.

Despite our evolution through three distinct variations of capitalism, the government's policy toward the environment has remained basically the same. It has never taken a firm and clear position on protecting the environment.

Under mercantilism, business existed at the whim of the government and for its benefit and was not free to pursue its own goals. The government's desire was not to protect nature but to exploit it through its business agents for the benefit of both parties, especially the government. Nationalism, not conservation, was the primary moving force behind such policies. Even with the advent of laissez faire, when the government eased out of its direct partnership with business, it still encouraged and cooperated with environmental exploitation that would benefit business and, by indirect means, the government and the nation as a whole. With the coming of the Great Depression and the welfare-state policies of the New Deal, government reasserted much of its authority over the economic life of the nation but seldom for the benefit of nature. Admittedly, some New Deal measures, such as the Agricultural Adjustment Administration, had conservation as a stated goal, but this was too often used as a political technique to get around possible constitutional limitations on the exercise of federal power. There were indeed environmental benefits from such legislation, but they were mostly additional or unexpected dividends from programs operating from different motivations. Indeed, with conscious efforts toward that goal, the environment could have benefited enormously. But, whatever has been the public policy of our government throughout the past, the environment, unfortunately, has been the loser.

Despite this statement, one finds an historically confusing record. Very often government policy has been definitely anti-nature while at other times (unfortunately, too rare) it has taken a strong stand. Too often the record has been ambiguous.

One of the prime examples among the most criticized policies in recent years has been the government's farm program. Admittedly, the government has faced such an unprecedented dilemma in the past hundred years, one that never seemed possible before, that to develop a rational approach and solution requires much ingenuity. Simply put, the problem has been an overabundance of farm products; American farmers, in truth, have been too good at their jobs. Faced with such an unexpected situation, government and private groups have struggled to solve it, with little success; the most that can be said is that the disastrous economic consequences of overproduction were finally mitigated to some extent.

From its first appearance in the 1880s until the 1920s, most Americans simply refused to admit that the situation really existed. The very idea that we were producing more food than we could use was considered simply preposterous by most people. They could always point to hungry people and conclude that distribution, wages, or employment opportunities were at fault. Then, when the depression of the thirties made the existence of hungry people an everyday fact of life, it was more than credibility could stand to be told again that we regularly produced too much.

Responses during this fifty-year period varied. Populists and other farm protest groups in the 1880s and 1890s believed that the problem was not overproduction but such things as low prices, high freight rates, or foreign competition. Particularly, they blamed the general troubles on the financiers of "Wall Street" (a term of severe opprobrium) who, they believed, controlled world and domestic markets, credit, and the lives of individuals. Such charges were comfortable for those who accepted the conspiracy theory of history, and it did personify the problem in one man—J. P. Morgan—or a small group of people—Wall Street bankers. Yet, despite the various factors the farmers believed responsible for their problems, they were hard-pressed to deny or ignore the excess crops in storage.

Not until the 1920s was the problem recognized for what it really was. At that time various proposals were made, not for controlling prices or setting freight rates, but for disposing of the surplus products by using various governmental and available private agencies. The most meaningful proposal was embodied in the McNary-Haugen bills introduced and passed through Congress on several occasions only to be vetoed by unsympathetic presidents. The McNary-Haugen approach was significant in several ways. For the first time the country publicly admitted the existence of overproduction. The legislators conceived scarcity in worldwide terms. The ingrained American Protestant ethic concerning work and production was, or seemed to be, set aside. The federal government was clearly accepted as the only agency or institution capable of coping with such a massive problem. Although the bills did not become law, the very fact that they could pass Congress meant that more and more people were forced to face reality. Thus, in effect, Congress went on record as accepting the premise of governmental responsibility, and, to a very large extent, set the stage for the massive federal involvement that came under the leadership of Franklin Roosevelt.

Despite the forward-looking nature of the McNary-Haugen proposals, they still reflected one basic misunderstanding and practical weakness. Instead of providing for the prevention of future agricultural surpluses, the bills would have arranged only for eliminating current surpluses, in this case by dumping them on the world market without consideration of the consequences. The idea of limiting the amount of a crop to be produced was not added until the thirties.

In all the debate over the farm problem, there was almost no environmental concern expressed. Although the damage done by many staple crops to the soil had been well known since colonial times, few people seemed to recognize that the soil could be restored and surpluses eliminated through a centralized planning of soil utilization. Such objectives were the stated goals of the AAA in the thirties. Even so, there was more obvious concern for the economic benefit from eliminating surpluses than there was in protecting the soil; and some have questioned the program's real success toward either goal.

Most often, historically, the government was more concerned about economic prosperity than about the condition of nature.

The same attitude was always true in the history of the government's policy toward land utilization in the United States. Most of the government was more concerned with getting unused land into the hands of private owners who would develop it rather than with seeing that it be utilized properly. Although there were many occasions when land was simply thrown open to wild and unplanned settlement, such as Indian Territory (Oklahoma) in 1889, there were a few occasions when careful planning preceded settlement. One of the most praised and usually considered successful programs of the federal government was the Ordinance of 1785. Enacted while the government was still operating under the Articles of Confederation, this law provided for the orderly distribution of land in what was then called the Northwest Territory, today the states of Ohio, Indiana, Illinois, Wisconsin, and Michigan. Arrangements were made for a survey and subdivision of the land that would then be offered at public auction. The goal was to make relatively small plots of land available to small farmers at reasonable prices. In addition, the law made provisions for public education, among other things. This law remained the basic, although often drastically modified, model by which land was distributed in other parts of the country. But, even though the federal government was very much involved, no arrangements were made to protect the environment or natural resources. The use of timber, minerals, and water resources was left to the individual landowners as it always had been in this country. Action to protect these resources very seldom occurred to anyone, since there was no recognition of a need. Settlement and development were considered so necessary to the whole country that the first thought and order of business was to exploit the resources available. Even had the need been recognized, the prevailing belief in a limited government would probably have required that any action to protect nature should originate from private sources.

In the late nineteenth century when the pressure was

very strong for settling the land as rapidly as possible, the federal government helped in every way it could. There were times, however, when government action was concerned with the condition of the soil. Not that the government attempted to restrict settlement; just the reverse was true. However, the government was concerned that land be in the hands of small farmers and that it be as fertile and as useful as possible. During the 1870s the federal government passed three laws designed to achieve these goals.

The Timber Culture Act of 1873 made available 160 acres of land to anyone who would plant one-fourth of it in trees. In 1878 the requirement was reduced to ten acres. The rationale behind this law was the hope that trees would somehow slow the constant winds of the plains and would, at the same time, attract more rainfall and retain more of its moisture. According to some cynics, the real motivation behind the law was the unwillingness of eastern Congressmen to accept the fact that nature had not intended trees to grow on the plains. Possibly, they believed that forests could be created in the West by legislating them. The tree requirement most often was ignored, but in the instances where the farmer obeyed the law, the trees never did very well. Yet under this law over nine million acres were distributed.

The Desert Land Act of 1877 provided that 640 acres could be obtained for a down payment of twenty-five cents per acre. Within three years the owner was required to bring at least part of the land under irrigation, at which time he could pay an additional one dollar per acre and receive full title. Later evidence shows that the land involved was not desert at all, but instead was good grazing land. The pressure for its passage came from ranchers who wanted more cheap grazing land. In addition to being the cause of much fraud and dishonesty, the law also reflected the lack of understanding about the costs and other requirements involved in artificially irrigating land. Later efforts have shown that massive irrigation projects are among the most costly and risky ventures that can be undertaken. Nevertheless, the Desert Land Act distributed over 2½ million acres.

The Timber and Stone Act of 1878 allowed the sale of land "unfit for cultivation" to private interests for $2.50 per acre. The idea was that the land was valuable only for its timber and stone. Through this very large legal loophole, virgin timber resources were sold for a pittance to private companies that proceeded rapidly to denude much of the West.

Even though these three laws appear to have had a concern for the environment, their application worked just the reverse. Even if the government were sincere in its concern, events of the time showed that a basically weak and limited government was no match for the powerful private interests. Some students have suggested that the laws were not meant to protect nature. These provisions they think, were written into the laws to make them look good and to get the necessary Congressional support while, in fact, they were so loosely written that they could be easily abused, as they truly were. Whatever one's verdict may be, the government, obviously, did not make much progress in protecting the environment at this stage of development.

One other action of the federal government shows the ambiguity of federal conservation measures. With the strong support of President Theodore Roosevelt in 1902, Congress passed the Newlands Act, which provided that a proportion of the revenue from the sale of public lands would be used for conservation projects in the West—especially the construction of dams and reclamation projects. The one resource to be conserved was the water that daily emptied out of the mountains and plains into the ocean without benefit to man, or so it seemed. Dams would hold this water until it could be properly utilized for irrigation; little concern was evident for the ecological impact that impounding great quantities of water would have. Once again, even if conservation were the ostensible motivation, the real benefit of such legislation was economic.

Care should be taken here to emphasize that these

comments are not meant as criticism of the laws. The motivation behind them in most instances was of the highest quality. In retrospect, they may seem highly idealistic and simplistic solutions to the utilization of land that nature had intended for purposes other than farming. Today, of course, we know more about the problems created by such projects. The damage done to the fertile land in the Colorado River valley on the Mexican side of the border by excessive saline deposits that have made the land useless is a good example. The primary purpose of these examples is to show that the government's commitment to conservation has not been very strong; far too often the government used the name of conservation as a means of enacting legislation that had a far different purpose and impact.

A discussion of conservation brings to the surface the existence of two diverging points of view about what conservation really is—one eastern and the other western—that created serious difficulties in the twentieth century. The eastern attitude, molded to a large extent by the influence of the Yale School of Forestry, considered conservation to be mostly preservation. Extreme care should be exercised, this group believed, when using nature's bounties, because most of them could never be replaced and replacement, in any case, would take far too long. Therefore, exploitation should be cautious and slow. Of course, this view was not commonly held by all Americans living in the East; it was here, after all, that some of the worst exploitation took place in providing for the insatiable appetite of industry's machines. Yet, among those in the East interested in conservation, preservation seemed to be the key word.

In the West the attitude was somewhat different. Most westerners seemed little concerned about conservation, but among those who were, the prevailing attitude was that conservation meant an orderly and systematic use of the bounties of nature. Trees and underground mineral deposits were of questionable value if they remained undisturbed by man. Fertile soil was of little value without water, and the rivers and streams should not be allowed to carry the unused, precious liquid to the sea without regulation. Thus, controlled and wise utilization was synonymous with conservation. This attitude is still very widely held in the West today. A few years ago when environmentalists were protesting the proposed lumbering of the few remaining redwood forests in California, certain leaders, unable to understand their concern, responded by saying, "When you have seen one redwood you have seen them all." Although some may deplore such an attitude, it has been a large part of the western mentality (although not limited exclusively to that area) which sees profit and material benefits as more important than beauty or long-term environmental balance. When reminded by critics that the wholesale cutting of forests also results in flooding, erosion, destruction of wildlife, and a more restricted life style, such leaders usually reply, or imply, that flooding and erosion can be controlled by other means and that the other disadvantages are simply a part of the price society pays for progress.

This diverging East-West point of view about the environment or conservation has often given the federal government the appearance of a schizophrenic personality. Too often the government, in an attempt to satisfy its varied constituencies and to placate powerful political interests, tries to be all things to all men. Therefore, it is not uncommon for the government to promote environmental protection on the one hand and cooperate with or encourage its despoliation on the other. Such was the case a few years ago when the government purchased and stored surplus eggs to support prices received by the egg producer, while at the very same time the same agency of the government was making loans to persons going into the egg production business. Such inconsistencies result, in part, from the attempts to please all people, but they also result, in large measure, from the massive bureaucracy, mentioned earlier, one part of which is often unaware or unconcerned about the actions of another part.

Probably one of the best examples of the government's

split personality was the so-called Ballinger-Pinchot controversy, mentioned earlier in these pages. Gifford Pinchot, a disciple of the eastern conservation school, considered himself, as the head of the Forest Service, to be the defender of trees. Any widespread attempt to lumber the forests immediately faced his wrath. Richard Ballinger, his immediate superior as secretary of agriculture, was a follower of the western concept of conservation. Therefore, when Ballinger allowed national forests to be used for commercial purposes by private firms, the stage was set for a controversy that had long and serious political repercussions. Pinchot lost the battle, but his defeat did not mean that the federal government had fallen under the domination of the western interests. It meant simply that the government had no specific attitude or policy toward the environment and dealt with each situation or crisis in the context of current political realities.

In truth, the government, in environmental matters, reacted only when there was a public outcry against a policy that endangered the environment. When the public was quiet and complacent (most of the time), environmental spoliation continued without government restriction and often with its tacit approval and encouragement. The same trends are apparent today. President Nixon's proposals to Congress and subsequent legislation to protect the environment would not have occurred, it seems likely, had there not been a growing public concern about the state of the environment. For several years, beginning probably with the publication of Rachel Carson's *Silent Spring* in the early sixties, the number of alarmed people grew significantly to the culminating point in the Earth Day observances in 1970. A major factor was Miss Carson's book, together with others of the same type, which began to force a public realization that as a nation (and planet) we are reaching the end of the time when nature can be abused with impunity. With such a sentiment growing, it became politically safe for political leaders to appear as the vocal champions of environmental protection even though their private actions did not always match their public utterances. Again, the suspicion lingers in the mind of the environmentalist that the government is not serious in its stated goals.

Environmentalists believe that if popular sentiment returns to its normal apathetic state, then the government will gradually ease its restrictions and allow the environment to become once again the plaything of those interests who benefit from its spoliation. Those who are concerned are fearful that the protection of the environment will face a future similar to that of the civil rights movement and the demands for racial justice. Since the violence associated with black activism and the rising agitation over the Vietnam war in the mid-sixties caused civil rights activity to go off in many directions, often leaderless after the death of Martin Luther King in 1968, the government has modified its policies and deferred many strong efforts to provide equal rights for all Americans. Today, of course, the future of government policy toward racial justice is very unclear. The environmentalists fear that the same can happen to the ecology movement if the pressure and vigilance are ever relaxed or if another major public issue should arise to deflect public concern as Vietnam did from civil rights. Unfortunately, they have many precedents to buttress their fears.

Not only has the government been ambivalent in its attitude; there have been specific instances of governmental indifference, and specific agencies that have taken a very antiecological position. Although numerous examples could be given, one of the most heavily criticized agencies of the federal government in this regard is the Army Corps of Engineers. Under foreign wartime combat conditions, the Corps performed feats that were considered virtually impossible. They were able to construct facilities almost overnight that quite often meant the difference between victory and defeat. It might seem unpatriotic to question such valuable wartime activities, but it is important to remember that even those heroic examples of success were often quite damaging to the environment, possibly because the Corps acted under emergency conditions. War is, of course, a special and hopefully abnormal condition, and one is more likely at such times to tolerate actions that he would not normally endorse. The critics contend that the Corps was very unconcerned about the consequences of its actions and that it has used much the same methods in many of its projects in this country. No one should be misled to believe that the Corps is totally disliked; it has its many defenders both within and without the government, who believe that the organization has been a major, positive force in developing this country. Nonetheless, the Corps has often been the center of great controversy.

Among the most controversial of the Corps' activities is its emphasis on dam building. In most of the projects a major justification has been conservation of water resources. By building dams on untamed rivers, its leaders claim, water and wildlife as well as property are saved from periodic destruction. Additional benefits include increased navigational possibilities, recreation facilities, flood control, and hydroelectric facilities. The Corps' defenders can point to numerous examples, such as the TVA, where the benefits are obvious. Few would argue that these goals are undesirable, but the critics claim that the overall liabilities of many proposed projects are greater than the assets. The Corps, they claim, seldom takes into consideration the disruption of the delicate ecological balance that exists in an area prior to the construction. Often this balance is totally disrupted, leaving instead a desolate condition or a radically altered ecosystem. In addition, the dams are sometimes so improperly planned that there is not enough water to fill the projected lake, or the silting is so bad that the lakes fill up behind the dams, necessitating massive and constant dredging resulting in the uselessness of the dams and the lakes, which become bogs or swamps. Admittedly, these criticisms are harsh and possibly exaggerated, but, without question, proposals made by the Corps often create much local hostility.

Among the more controversial projects of the Corps was the proposed building of a dam in the Red River valley of Kentucky. In a remote area of east central Kentucky, this is one of the most scenic and beautiful, even primitive, areas in the eastern United States. Within the gorge created by the river are some beautiful and unique specimens of trees, flowers, and wildlife. The project proposed by the Corps and originally approved by Congress in 1962 provided for an artificial lake that would fill most of the gorge and probably destroy much of the rest of it. Critics argued that the Corps' stated goals of flood control, electric power, and recreation were falsely assumed since the danger from flooding was minimal, sufficient electric power was already available from TVA dams and other electric plants in the area, and recreation facilities were already abundant in the region. One benefit, accepted even by the critics, was that the lake would provide water for Lexington and other downstream communities.

The dam did not become a public issue until the late sixties when the Sierra Club and other conservationist groups became involved. In order to dramatize the situation and hopefully obtain a reversal of the decision, Supreme Court Justice William O. Douglas and his wife hiked through the area with newspaper reporters and photographers who reported the natural beauties that would be lost if it were covered by a lake. Governor Louie B. Nunn then joined the opposition. Finally, in 1971 a compromise was announced that would move the dam far enough downstream, it was believed, to prevent serious ecological damage. By early 1973 the project was still in the planning stages, since Congress had not appropriated money for actual construction. In addition, new federal laws require the Corps of Engineers to prepare an environmental-impact statement before any major construction project is started. While environmentalists seemed somewhat satisfied with the compromise, they were withholding judgment until the report was available. Ironically enough, during the years of controversy the gorge received so much publicity that today it is threatened by destruction by the hordes of tourists that have been attracted to it.[4]

Some might truthfully say that the Corps of Engineers is only one agency, that it is not representative of overall governmental policy, but there are enough examples of this sort available to make it fairly certain that the government has very seldom had a stated or firm policy on environmental protection. Of course, it is also very true that the federal government is not the only villain here. State and local governments have been as bad, if not worse, in some of their actions.

One of the most ambitious schemes ever devised was the proposal by the state of Texas to divert a major portion of the Mississippi River to Texas. Facing a future water shortage, particularly in agricultural and industrial development, Texas devised a plan whereby the water of the Mississippi would be diverted at its mouth and transported across Louisiana through a series of dams, canals, and holding pools into east Texas. There it would be added to the "surplus" water from east Texas streams and transported to west and south Texas where the greatest needs are. This was a very complicated plan that would require the building of a concrete canal some 800 miles long and the pumping of more than 13 million acre-feet of water over 3,000 feet uphill, requiring some 6 million kilowatts of electricity. Water would be collected in east Texas reservoirs that would cover an area roughly the size of the state of Connecticut. The cost to the state would be $3.5 billion, and to the federal government, $6.5 billion. The plan was much more complex and massive than this brief summary shows, but the statements that it was "the biggest bond issue in the history of the world,"[5] and that it would "provide for the largest altering of the face of the earth ever undertaken by man"[6] give some indication of its significance.

This proposal provoked one of the most vocal and serious debates in many years. Defenders said that it was the answer to the state's problems. Since farm land in some areas would have a dependable water supply for the first time, production would undoubtedly rise. Much of the agricultural productivity of the Texas high plains would be destroyed in twenty to fifty years unless the diminishing supply of water could be restored. Large amounts of water would also be available for the first time for existing industry and for the attraction and development of new industries. Among the greatest hindrances to industrial growth had always been inadequate water; this plan, they claimed, could bring a new age of boom to the state.

Opponents were just as vocal. Most of the opposition came because of the cost of the project. This, they claimed, would put the state in debt for generations without any guarantees that the amount of water it produced would be adequate. Environmentalists were particularly upset by the dangers they could envision if the project were carried out. The redirection of much of the Mississippi would create havoc in the Gulf of Mexico, now to be deprived of its normal water flow; in Louisiana the new canal would upset the normal environmental balance, and in Texas the long-range impact could only be guessed. The containing of surplus stream water, the opponents claimed, would destroy the bays and estuaries where a proper mixture of salt and fresh water is needed to provide for marine life. The water imported from the Mississippi would be polluted since it would have already been used several times before it reached Texas. Although nothing specific could be predicted, most scientists agreed that there would be some climatological changes. In truth, the environmentalists argued, to carry out such a project would be to invite ecological disaster. As one opponent put it, Texans were asked "to approve a giant game of ecological Russian Roulette!"[7] Supporters of the plan claimed that one of the major concerns embodied in the proposal was to study the ecological impact. Yet the opponents contended that such studies had been inadequate at best and deliberately deceiving at worst. The debate waxed long and hot before the voters of Texas went to the polls in August, 1969.

The bond issue to finance the plan was defeated by some six thousand votes in 1969, a rather uncomfortable margin for environmentalists. Although there is no way to prove motivation, the issue was probably defeated as much for its projected costs as for anything else. Even though they were unable to make the public fully aware of the ecological dangers, the environmentalists were happy, at least, that they and other opponents were able to defeat the measure on the issue of cost. The opponents of the plan soon learned, however, that it may not have been a permanent victory. Supporters of the plan were not completely crushed, since the margin had been so close. In addition, recent reports show that the plan is being carried out piecemeal by the state through selected construction of dams and reservoirs that may eventually complete the larger plan.[8]

This proposal is a very good example of the ambiguity that exists at the state level. In this instance, state government promoted a plan that, if not destructive of nature, at least offered the potential. The primary question, of course, is what is in the best public interest. Is the development of economic potential (progress?) more important than the environment? How does one strike a balance between the economic necessities on one hand and the quality of life that economic growth influences on the other? These are valid and serious questions that cannot be avoided indefinitely, and, in the final analysis, answers are very much political.

Among the most obvious areas of conflict between the two positions is the proposed channelization of streams promoted today by both the federal and state governments and supported by the Corps of Engineers. This is a process by which the natural current and bed of rivers and streams are dredged to widen and deepen them and to straighten them if possible for navigation purposes. Environmentalists, appalled by such proposals, say that such a process makes formerly beautiful and scenic streams into little more than muddy ditches. Not only does the channelization destroy much of the natural flora and fauna, but it also intensifies pollution damage by making possible more extensive navigation and potential spills of cargo. In addition to the loss of natural beauties, channelization disrupts the ecological balance, which threatens to alter the human life style just as it destroys much of nature. Alarmed environmentalists have a nightmarish vision of a time when virtually all waterways will have been destroyed.

One of the most ambitious channelization proposals is, once again, in Texas. The Trinity River, which passes through Dallas and Fort Worth, has long been considered a potential water route to the Gulf of Mexico. Supporters claim that a complicated series of dams and reservoirs, and massive amounts of stream dredging and straightening, can make Dallas and Fort Worth among the most important inland seaports in the world. A brief examination of the project reveals its scope. The Trinity River is approximately 550 miles long. The new waterway would be a 335-mile channelized stream, little more than a ditch with much stone and concrete construction, that would require three reservoirs, a floodway, and numerous high bridges along the route.

Critics contend that one of the primary motivations is the rivalry between Dallas and Houston. The fifty-mile-long channel which allows Houston to be the second largest port in the country has been one of the major stimulants to the city's phenomenal growth. However, opponents believe that the two projects should be compared closely and the lessons provided by the Houston channel should be emphasized. For example, the Houston channel is only 50 miles long, while the proposed Trinity canal would be 335 miles long. Anyone who has seen the open sewer that the Houston channel has become, they say, should be appalled by the prospect of a similar ecological disaster some 335 miles long.

The future of the Trinity project is unclear. Congress approved the plan in 1965, but there seems to be some hesitation now to fund it. The federal government may be backing away from the massive financial contribution that it normally makes to such projects. Opponents of the plan are hopeful that the prospect of total state and local financing will defeat the actual construction. Unfortunately, they realize that, as with the Texas Water Plan, costs are more often a deterrent than potential ecological disaster.[9]

The project is not dead, however. Just as the opposition mounts, so does the support. The proposal has major political support, such as that of Congressman Jim Wright of Fort Worth. One of his statements reflects a concern that has been expressed over and over again in these pages: "The environment exists primarily to accommodate the human species. The Earth exists for man, not the other way around."[10] There is nothing essentially wrong with the statement as it stands; the way in which the earth is made to accommodate the human species is the question. If that means the destruction of nature for questionable economic gains, then it becomes a matter of concern. If such an attitude is widely held by government officials, then realistic protection of the environment becomes even more difficult.

Perhaps one other example will suffice to show that the federal government's attitude toward the environment is little different today than in the past. During the 1950s the interstate highway system was planned and construction was started. In order to get Congressional approval and to overcome possible constitutional limitations, the system was designated a matter of national defense as an evacuation system in case of foreign attack or other national emergencies. The fact that it had to be justified through a subterfuge might well have been warning enough. Should it not have been simple enough to say that the transportation system was so overcrowded that a new system was needed for the general welfare? Obviously, in the context of that day, approval of defense measures was obtained almost automatically.

The interstate system is long past its originally targeted completion date. As delays developed and construction costs mounted, the completion date was repeatedly set back. Gradually, also, the size of the system was expanded far beyond its original scope to accommodate more cities and to penetrate virtually every area of the country. The system is now nearing completion, but it has proved to be a very costly undertaking.

Most anyone who uses an interstate highway is impressed by its efficiency. Distances and travel time have been reduced significantly. Overall, the system is a safer one, despite improper engineering and construction on some portions that were so poorly done that they became traffic hazards and had to be corrected. Thus, as far as the original purposes of the system were concerned, little fault could be found. However, it is the environment, an aspect of the project almost totally neglected in the planning stages, that has suffered.

In some areas construction of the interstate system virtually remade the environment. Massive amounts of land were taken, far more than necessary according to some complaints. There are those, in fact, who believe that the nation is in danger of being covered over with asphalt and concrete and that the interstate system is the major culprit. In addition, many trees were destroyed, with the usual resulting damage to wildlife and surrounding soil. The highways have changed the grades, thus altering the normal drainage systems. In many cases, the drainage has been completely redirected and has caused damage to nearby private property. The critics contend that the obsession in the system for nationwide standardization has encouraged construction practices that have been very harmful to nature.

Various other examples could be used to show that government, at any level, has virtually no coherent, reasonable attitude about the environment. Government is a part of the political system and thus changes with the political winds. To expect anything less would be naive. Governmental leaders are politicians who take strong stands only when necessary, since the potential adverse public reaction could be personally damaging. In short, politicians usually are not very brave souls; the few that are often find their careers rather short-lived.

If the environmentalist hopes to bring about significant change, he must recognize that one of his major obstacles, and often outspoken opponents, will be the government. He must also recognize that even if he obtains a favorable government attitude, it will often be a temporary one.

The problem is to find somehow a governmental system that can do the right thing despite adverse public opinion. A truly responsive government is necessary. But when government takes a strong stand on environmental protection, it will face an extremely hostile business community.

The answers to the problem are ill-defined. It may well be that our government as presently constituted is not capable of meeting the challenges of the environment and other issues of the seventies. It may be that the government needs a massive overhaul, or it may need only slight modifications. The first urgent need is an unimpassioned study of our system to see if it is capable of meeting these challenges. Alterations or modifications may be proposed which will totally change the system. Those who undertake such an examination will not get far if they are met with emotional responses that brand them as disloyal or subversive. Obviously, some examination must come. It may bring a political revolution, but that is one of the possibilities that must be faced.

6

THE POPULATION REVOLUTION

Throughout American history the concept of growth has been one of the most widely held values. From the first faltering steps on the North American shores at Jamestown and Plymouth until the very recent past, rapid growth in every sense —physical, economic, population—has been considered necessary for survival. As the nation enlarged its geographic boundaries, its economic position grew; with the resulting demands, the pressures for a larger population were intense.

Growth became an almost sacred concept to Americans, and to a large extent, to the industrialized West. Size became synonymous with power, strength, prosperity, self-respect. Anyone who suggested that growth was not desirable was merely short-sighted or, at worst, subversive. Any nation with a small population and a desire for industrialization seemed doomed to failure, since productive growth required numerous people, as both laborers and customers. American cities, until very recently at least, waited anxiously for each federal census report so that they could proclaim with great pride their anticipated, unprecedented growth. Some cities, unable to contain their enthusiasm and wait for the official count, took their own surveys and proudly posted the estimated populations on signs leading into the city and any other appropriate place. Not uncommonly some of them were forced to revise their estimates to conform to the true picture revealed by the official census taker. Even so, some cities suggested that the official census was inaccurate for various reasons, so strong was the desire for growth.

This obsession with size and growth has afflicted almost all segments of American life. After World War II colleges and universities were inundated with students, reflecting the growing demand for higher education by a larger percentage of an ever-growing population. College administrators, rather than being embarrassed by the unprecedented demands, often boasted of overcrowding and lack of facilities. Sometimes their claims were exaggerated, possibly to encourage more public and private aid to meet the new needs. Additions to existing facilities were built as rapidly as plans could be drawn and financing obtained. Individual campuses proudly announced record-breaking enrollments each year, and state systems, now with a very effective lobby in state legislatures, were quick to announce the establishment of new institutions to meet the new demands even though some were hastily and improperly planned. Sources of private and public funds were strained by the new pressures for financial aid, but few people complained of the burden in the heyday of optimistic growth. Some critics complained that college bureaucratic growth was a perfect example of Parkinson's Law at work, but even so, most of the expansion seemed necessary and worth the cost because enrollments did increase, and modern, quality education was expensive. By the late sixties and early seventies, some administrators were forced to take second looks and to admit grudgingly that they may have overbuilt during the days of great optimism.

Obsession with size has been the watchword of all institutions and of our thought processes generally. Churches proclaim that they are the largest in a city, state, or nation. We talk about the most production, the largest work force, the largest state. We are, in truth, a nation possessed by a desire to be the best, the most, or the largest. Records are important to us in all respects; the records with most adherents are those that concern size. Overall, this is an ingrained concept that may well be one of the most difficult to dislodge, particularly in regard to changing environmental attitudes.

After 350 years of national preoccupation with the goals of size, the environmentalist must recognize that this may be the most difficult attitude he will face. Growth has meant progress, position, and power; smaller growth, or no growth at all, suggests an end to progress, a demotion in position, and decreasing power. Few Americans will readily accept such changes voluntarily.

The matter of population has been one where size and growth have been most destructive. Despite recent reports that the American birth rate has dropped to its lowest level in our history, the expected optimism should be very cautious, since trends have a way of reversing themselves almost without warning. There is certainly no guarantee that current figures represent a long-range trend; in fact, the birth rate could reverse itself overnight. Even a few years of increased births could create environmental havoc, since the impact of only slightly increased populations in industrialized countries is so much greater than the actual numbers would suggest.

As environmentalists have already learned, the job of convincing Americans to limit population growth is a most difficult task, despite the apparent present decline in the birth rate. Thus, a major part of the revolution will be to force the awareness of population dangers upon those who do not already recognize them and to keep the issue constantly before the public. One must recognize, of course, that action of this sort conflicts not only with ingrained habits, but also with social, religious, and ethical considerations. Obviously, the task of the environmentalist is not easy.

Since Paul Ehrlich[1] has already explained very adequately the dangers of excessive population, there is no need here to restate his arguments. There does seem to be a need, however, to summarize a few of his points because they are very much related to the other issues to be raised.

As Ehrlich says, the American people hold many misconceptions about world population. Americans travel throughout their country and discover wide open, virtually uninhabited areas and conclude that the problem of overpopulation must be exaggerated. One might expect to find open territory in the West, but not unexpectedly, much of it would not be inhabitable except under extreme conditions. One of the most shocking discoveries for many westerners is to visit the Northeast (and contrary to the provincial attitude of many of those in the East, the Northeast, to southerners and westerners, usually means everything north of the Ohio River and east of about Indiana or Ohio) and discover that there are many rural, almost wild, areas there. After all, for people who have never visited the Midwest and Northeast, it is very easy to believe that the area is nothing more than an unbroken urban-industrial jungle as movies and television would lead us to believe. Thus, a rather broad cross section of the American people tends to believe that there is space in the country for double or triple our current population.

Of course, the problem is not related entirely to numbers. It is complicated by the fact that increasing populations do not spread out onto the poor or unusable land; the new people take some of the most fertile acreage in the country. Population growth is not rational and does not utilize land which is least valuable for agriculture. Thus, just at a time when the pressure on food production increases, the most productive land is covered by asphalt and concrete to provide living space and accommodations for increasing numbers of people. When one adds to that the other population-related developments, such as highways and airports with their insatiable appetites for land, it is easier to see that the space requirements for an expanded population concern more than just the few square feet that the individual privately uses.

Additionally, the American seems to think that the most serious population problems are in large countries such as China or India. Few would minimize the importance of the birth rate in those countries, but once again Ehrlich has separated myth from fact. Actually, the child born in the United States today does enormously more damage to the environment than he would were he born in one of the underdeveloped nations. Because he is born into an urban industrial nation, his very existence puts more strain on natural resources, demands more services, and utilizes more facilities. As a result, even though our birth rate is lower than in many parts of the world, we do much more damage to the environment. Again, to use Ehrlich's figures, the United States with 1/15 of the world's population uses over one-half of its resources; at present rates Americans, within twenty years, will use approximately 80 percent of the resources even though the population will be a smaller proportion of the world's total. In addition, the industrialized nation does much more to foul the environment. Each new resident adds more to air and water pollution than numerous persons in other places simply because he adds more to the demands which cause these problems.

Therefore, as Ehrlich points out, the crucial area for population control is in the United States and other industrialized nations. Admittedly, the underdeveloped part of the world must bring its population under control simply for survival and decent living standards, but their numbers do not present the clear and present danger to the environment that those in the industrialized West do. Thus, it is really the West which has the most urgent problem and whose long-held views must be changed most rapidly. Furthermore, since it is supposedly wrong to meddle in the affairs of other countries, we must face the problem in our own country where we have the most possibility of achieving results. But before significant change in ideas can come, we must understand those ideas and their origins.

America, as already noted, was born in a spirit of optimism and a belief in progress. With the obvious natural wealth available here and the unlimited space, population anxieties never occurred to the early settlers. Even when Thomas Malthus[2] published his book *Essay on Population* in

1798, few if any Americans gave it any attention. Eventually Malthus became quite a controversial figure, but his conclusions and predictions never really concerned Americans until the very recent past.

Despite the indifference of the Americans, Malthus had several important things to say to them, then and now. Essentially, he said that the population increases in geometric progression while the food supply increases in simple arithmetic progression. If he were to prove correct, every part of the world would be faced with possible or, more likely, probable chaos. Even in newly opened areas like North America, the food supply diminishes more rapidly as the population grows larger. Therefore, although Americans might look back smugly and assume that they had escaped the congestion and poverty of Europe, if Malthus were to be believed, the United States would have to face the same situation, given enough time. In fact, the very prosperity, real or potential, of colonial America encouraged another trend which Malthus foresaw. An abundance in the food supply, he said, only encouraged a more rapid procreation. As the population increased from such a stimulus, the enlarged numbers would eventually force the population back to the subsistence level or lower since the food supply would be used up.

Again, if Malthus were to prove correct, what was to keep the population from being destroyed as the food supply eventually disappeared? Certainly, if his theory were carried far enough, that result would seem to be the logical conclusion. He answered that there are certain checks on the population such as war, pestilence, starvation, abortion, and infanticide. In fact, he said, those things had all occurred in the past to keep the population under control and thus explained its continued existence. These are, of course, negative checks on the population, but he said that there was also one positive check—total abstinence from sexual intercourse.

Another question raised about his theories was whether this was an absolute law; could something be done to prevent the disaster that he predicted? After all, his ideas laid the groundwork for David Ricardo's "Iron Law of Wages."[3] Published in 1817, Ricardo's theory carried Malthus even farther. He said that demands for higher pay for workers were useless for raising living standards since greater income only encouraged more marriages and increased births. The worker, now with more children to feed, was forced back to a subsistence level. In addition, the increased population which added more people to the work force had a depressing effect upon all society. The worker could not be helped; industry suffered from interference; the food supply was further diminished. Therefore, any attempt to raise the worker above subsistence levels was foolish; all society should recognize this reality and accept it. Ricardo's ideas were very much influenced by Malthus and the other classical economists who were saying similar things.

In examining Malthus (and Ricardo too), one finds an interesting contradiction in ideas prevalent at the time. Malthus wrote in and was a product of the eighteenth century at the time when the Enlightenment, the Age of Reason—which emphasized the innate goodness and the perfectibility of man —was reaching its most influential period. According to the ideas of the Enlightenment, one thing which made it possible for man to control his own destiny and to make progress was the search for and discovery of the "natural laws" which governed man's existence. Once man discovered these laws, he could adapt to them, work in harmony with them, and improve his lot in life. Yet Malthus was also proclaiming a natural law, but it was one that was extremely pessimistic and essentially contradicted this optimistic view. How did one reconcile these differences? He could either conclude that Malthus was incorrect or he could ignore him.

Most Americans simply ignored Malthus. He could not possibly be correct, they reasoned, if one was aware of the riches of North America. What he said might apply to Europe, but he could not possibly have included this part of the world in his predictions. Even if he did, the disaster that he predicted was so far away that little concern should be given to it. Therefore, the Americans continued their activities of building, developing, and populating North America.

In the late nineteenth century a new generation of Americans who rediscovered Malthus concluded that he had been wrong in his theories. Since this was a time of renewed determinism, it was not possible to dismiss him out of hand; instead the new determinists—social Darwinists—had to pick his theory apart until they found a flaw. They concluded that Malthus was essentially correct for the time in which he lived and worked. However, he could not be expected to foresee developments of the nineteenth century that would make his fears unfounded. He could not have known, for example, that the agricultural and industrial revolutions would make possible the creation of food and other products on a scale never before known to man while at the same time producing a standard of living for all segments of society—the worker included—that was decent and above the subsistence level. Therefore, Malthus was correct as far as he went, but America and the Industrial Revolution had proven him incorrect in the longer view of history. As a result, his theories were once again relegated to a footnote in history and economics textbooks as an example of the wonders of the Industrial Revolution.

In the post–World War II era Malthus once again underwent a revival. Not even in the dark days of the depression was there any widespread feeling that he might have been correct after all. At that time there was no shortage of food; it was simply improperly distributed. It was not the inability to produce that caused suffering; instead, it was caused by either heartless public officials or an outmoded economic system. The production of agricultural surpluses, begun much earlier, continued through the thirties and the second World War, then into the postwar era. Malthus, therefore, could not have been correct, it seemed, since population had grown enormously, but the food supply had grown even faster.

During the sixties, however, Americans discovered, rather belatedly, that what was considered to be a perennial agricultural surplus was rapidly disappearing. Large surpluses of some staples such as cotton, in the process of being replaced by synthetics and other fibers, remained, but the surpluses in foodstuffs were no longer excessive. Malthus was quickly studied again with the result that some people began to think that he may have been correct all along. Perhaps the time that he had predicted and that Americans had consistently ignored was finally coming to pass. Americans began to discover the declining supplies of coal, oil, gas, and other industrial resources. Artificial fertilization of land to maintain a constant production level came under question because of the increasing dangers, particularly in the heavily fertilized valleys of California, of nitrate poisoning.[4] DDT, once a wonder chemical for controlling agricultural pests, was suddenly discovered to be a serious threat to humans who were developing large deposits of it in their bodies from consuming vegetables sprayed with the insecticide. The world seemed to be caving in; Malthus was alive and a threat again.

Obviously, these newly discovered problems were complicated by a large and growing population. If there were fewer people, natural resources would not be so threatened and would last longer into the future; fewer people, requiring less food, would lessen the demand for artificial fertilizers or DDT. Now some Americans became concerned that they had ignored Malthus's warning for too long and might soon become the victims of his predictions.

Despite the growing awareness today of Malthus and population problems generally, Americans have very seldom been concerned about excessive growth. American history is replete with examples of the reverence for large families. Several factors have contributed to this attitude.

Among the major forces encouraging large families was the religious motivation. At least two scriptural references could be found that encouraged rapid procreation. The first, already mentioned earlier in another context, can be found in the biblical description of creation. After God had created man and woman, He "blessed them and God said unto them,

Be fruitful and multiply, and replenish the earth . . ." (Genesis 1:28). Later, after all but Noah and his family had been destroyed in the Great Flood, God admonished Noah as he was about to leave the ark, "Bring forth with thee every living thing that is with thee, of all flesh, both of fowl, and of cattle, and of every creeping thing that creepeth upon the earth; that they may breed abundantly in the earth, and be fruitful, and multiply upon the earth" (Genesis 8:17). Thus, if one wished to interpret it that way, God made it a responsibility of man not only to reproduce his own kind, but to increase his numbers as well.

In a Protestant America such commands fell on fertile ground. In addition to an economic need for a large population, it was also godly to have many children. The indulging in sensual pleasures, the giving into one's carnal desires, was also justified, since the potential for conception was always present. Thus, man could convince himself that the real purpose of sexual intercourse, as many people interpreted it, was to create life; the physical pleasures that accompanied it were an added dividend, not the primary motive.

The obligation to produce children was accepted so completely in some instances in colonial America that serious consequences waited for those who were childless. A person who did not have children was considered an eccentric and, possibly, a deviant. It was a serious matter to disobey one of God's commands, but the social consequences were more immediate. The childless couple was often the object of scorn, ridicule, or pity. Usually the woman was blamed for a barren marriage; if afflicted with such apparent divine disfavor, the woman was given an additional burden that she had to bear gracefully. Even a childless couple that adopted children still bore the stigma of childlessness even though they might be considered good and humanitarian people for taking in children who had no other place to go. The question always remained as to why God did not favor them with the ability to produce.

A person who deliberately decided not to marry or who

waited longer than was socially acceptable was often looked upon as a burden or a parasite on society. Since he did not produce children and the associated economic growth, he was assumed not to be doing his share. Single persons seldom lived alone; out of necessity they often took subordinate positions— sometimes resembling a servant's—in the home of a relative. Studies of early American family patterns reveal that many households included a spinster sister, aunt, or cousin. Not uncommonly the community looked upon an unmarried person—especially a woman—as possibly the object of God's wrath for some unknown reason. Others were sometimes considered odd, even to the point of perversion and wickedness. Since a person's obligation to marry and produce children was a divine one, those who did not might be the agents of the devil. Interestingly, many of the people accused and tried for witchcraft in Salem, Massachusetts, were single women who lived alone and acted peculiarly. No one seemed to wonder if their strange behavior might have been due to the loneliness and isolation resulting from community ostracism for being unmarried. Thus, anyone without children, whether by choice or from biological limitations, was not easily made a part of society. The need for population growth was so important that private wishes could not be indulged; moreover, since procreation was divinely sanctioned, anyone who deliberately refrained from it was suspect.

Such an attitude has not totally disappeared today. A newly married couple today who voice the possibility that they may decide not to have children are sometimes shocked by the reactions they cause. They may be warned by family or friends that they have a Christian obligation to have children and that by refusing to do so they are risking divine displeasure. Even when they explain that the population has grown so large today that God's original command had been fulfilled, they may be answered by fundamentalist Protestants that in such a decision they are challenging God's word and possibly condemning themselves to perdition. If they try to discuss rationally the dangers of overpopulation and their unwillingness to add to the problem, such arguments will often fall on deaf ears. It is better, they are told, to do as the Bible says than to risk God's displeasure.

Protestants, of course, are not the only ones who hold such views about an increasing population. Catholics too have had much the same experience, only with a major difference. Protestants have not been able to develop any sort of unified attitude on the matter. Each Protestant group has been able to develop its own policy toward birth control. Many groups have simply left the whole matter to the consciences of the individual couple. Catholics, on the other hand, have had an official policy on the question, although the Church has had much difficulty, especially in recent years, in maintaining obedience to it.

Catholics, like many Protestants, have been told that having children is very much a part of God's plan. The emphasis on large families has been the source of much of the anti-Catholic sentiment that surfaced periodically throughout American history. Critics claimed that Catholics opposed birth control for other than religious reasons. They believed that it was a part of the Catholic conspiracy to increase Catholic population until it reached a majority status in this country, at which time the Church could dominate American affairs as it had done in Italy and other Catholic countries. First heard in the objections to Catholic immigration in the 1830s and 1840s, this charge has reemerged periodically even into the twentieth century. As late as 1928 and 1960, Catholic presidential candidates found themselves faced with the Protestant belief that their election would usher in papal rule in America even without an absolute Catholic majority.

Much of the controversy about limiting population growth has revolved around the difficulty in defining the precise moment when life begins. Catholics, more than Protestants, have been agitated by this question.

Catholic policy has never objected to birth control as long as it does not artificially prevent conception and the life resulting from it. Since the so-called rhythm method of birth control does not interfere, if used properly, with the normal biological reproductive process, it has been acceptable in the eyes of the Church. The problem, however, is to get a consensus on when life actually begins. Is an unborn fetus a living being at any time before birth? A person's age is dated from the moment of birth, not from conception, but one might argue that this is a legal distinction, not a theological one. If life begins before birth, then, as the Church maintains, to stop that life at any point is not only a crime, or should be, in the eyes of the law, but it is also a sin. Viewed in this perspective, the Church's stand on abortion is more easily understood. It, as well as many state laws, has been very rigid in determining the few abortions that are permissible. Although Malthus suggested this as one possibility, neither the Church nor the state has been willing to accept the practice of legal abortion as a means of population control.

Another area in which Catholics have been much more rigid than most Protestants is in the use of artificial contraceptive devices to prevent conception. The question of the life of an unborn fetus might be debatable, some say, but the Church's stand in opposing contraception has been questioned by many people, both Catholic and Protestant. They contend that it is unrealistic to say that the male sperm is itself life; thus, artificially to prevent it from fertilizing the female egg because this would destroy life (potential or conceived) is foolish. However, the Catholic Church, and some Protestants as well, have maintained that the primary purpose of sexual intercourse is to create life; any attempt to prevent it is wrong. Some have said that if one wishes to enjoy his sensual pleasures then he must also run the risk of pregnancy. Some have called this "population roulette."

Obviously, the ingrained American attitude about the proper function of population is important. If people are convinced of the religious necessity of large families, the environmentalist is, without question, faced with an enormous problem. However, the problem is even more difficult because American preferences for large populations are motivated by reasons that are broader and transcend religious convictions. A large population has always been considered a necessity in this country for personal economic reasons. We need to understand those as well.

As already stated, the American experience convinced most people from the very beginning that a large population was necessary for national growth and development. However, early colonial settlement was motivated by British nationalism, not American. The people who first settled this continent were motivated by personal reasons, but to the British, large and successful colonies would be of great international importance. She would be able to compete with the Spanish, especially since they were far advanced in that area. But weak, small, and struggling British colonies would probably be more a source of embarrassment than of pride. Thus, the colonies should grow and prosper. The first settlers, little concerned with British desires, took little note of population problems beyond their own immediate needs. Those first hardy souls who stepped into the wilderness soon recognized that they would have to increase their numbers rapidly or face the distinct possibility of becoming casualties to the New World environment just as earlier and smaller British attempts at colonial settlement had. When Jamestown and Plymouth experienced the so-called starving times during their first years of settlement when large percentages of the people died, they recognized immediately that the chances for survival of the whole settlement were quite bleak without large and rapid infusions of new residents.

After these very rough first years were behind them and permanency seemed assured, the British colonies began to look beyond their own boundaries. Something of a rivalry developed between the different British settlements; colonial outposts of other European nations in North America were also eyed enviously. Colonies with small populations could be in real danger of absorption by their larger neighbors; that fate befell the Plymouth colony, unable to hold out against the pressures of its larger and stronger neighbor, Massachusetts, and it was finally absorbed and its identity lost. The same fate eventually overtook the Dutch, Swedish, and Finnish settlements in North America. Because of their small sizes and weak positions, they were unable to resist their larger and more powerful British neighbors. Of course, the concern over population in this period was a recognition that they were too small rather than too large. It was some two or three hundred years later, however, before any serious national consciousness about excessive population growth developed.

As long as the United States remained a rural, agricultural nation, the birth rate was of little immediate concern to the individual. In order to create economic wealth and opportunity, the farmer had to farm as much land as possible, maintain as large a collection of farm animals as he could, and survive against the elements. In truth, he had to create his own capital since he brought little with him from Europe and most potential capital in this country was in a natural state. One of the most obvious ways he could create a place for himself was to have as large a family as possible who would aid him in this endeavor.

Before the days of machinery increased production depended upon as large a laboring force as possible. In the American South, African slavery seemed to be the answer for some, but, as studies have shown, the actual number of southerners who owned slaves were a very small proportion of the total southern population. The common misconception, perpetuated by novels and motion pictures, that virtually all white southerners were planters who lived a life of leisure based on the labor of blacks is simply not true. For the small farmer, north or south, the problem was to acquire labor one way or another as cheaply as he could. Only a man of some means could seriously entertain the prospect of becoming a slaveowner. Indentured white servitude was tried with debatable success; like slavery, it was an expensive proposition, often with more risk, and only a relatively small number of people were wealthy enough to take advantage of that source. Hired labor was also very scarce, even for those who could afford it. Usually a person forced to hire himself out had failed on his own and was a calculated risk for those who hired him. Therefore, for the average person struggling to obtain a share of the continent's wealth, the most logical way to acquire labor was to produce it himself.

In such a situation, the belief in and praise of large families is more easily understood. Records show that for many years the average family size was about ten children, with a few examples of twenty or more children born to the same mother. Admittedly, the infant mortality rate was high and the number of families with all children surviving to maturity was extremely small, but, in truth, the high death rate and the uncertainty of the future were all the more reasons to have as many children as practical.

Under such circumstances, children got little special attention; children were simply little people who had not yet grown to maturity. Childhood was merely the time, usually as short as posible, required to grow to the age when productive labor could be performed; psychology had not developed to the stage where childhood and adolescence were invented and children were recognized as unique creatures with their own special characteristics. The carefree childhood years were short; by the time a child was five or six years old, he began to shoulder his responsibilities. One should not be misled into believing that parents did not love their children, but the prevailing philosophy did not allow for the indulging of them. The major difference between then and now is that children played a special role in that earlier world, and, to a large extent, family survival and prosperity depended upon their fulfilling that role as soon as possible.

Social patterns were very much influenced by the attitudes toward family. The duty to marry and have children was not only for the benefit of the individual, but for society as well. Early marriage was the rule. In the twentieth century some observers have been alarmed by the increased numbers of teenage marriages. This may present problems for the contemporary world, but it is really nothing new; it is merely a return to a social pattern of an earlier day. In a period when it was not uncommon for a man to become a grandparent in his early thirties, the number of descendants that he could produce was literally astounding, as one learns when he studies some genealogical tables and family trees.

Divorce was hardly known in that early period. Not only were there religious sanctions against it, but, for the most part, it also put a person, especially a woman, outside the realm of decent society. Male dominance of society was very obvious in this attitude. Just as a woman was automatically blamed for a barren marriage, she was also, without obvious proof to the contrary, considered the guilty party in a divorce. In addition, a divorced person, male or female, did not really have a role in a society which automatically expected marriage and family as a normal state of affairs. For much the same reason, quick remarriage following death or divorce was the rule of the day. A woman left alone with children needed immediate assistance, and a man with children and a home needed a woman to see after his needs. There are recorded examples of arrangements for remarriage being made before, during, or shortly after the funeral of the departed mate. Long mourning periods were a luxury reserved for the wealthy and for a later day; the harsh realities of life required rapid action.

Large families had other benefits as well. Before the age of social security and a more enlightened social consciousness, a family was the only security a person had for old age; the larger the family, the more security there was. For a couple to have only one, two, or three children was to risk the distinct possibility that they would be left alone in old age with no means of support, either because of the uncertain longevity of their children or because their children might not be able, for one reason or another, to take care of them. Today this retirement feature of family life has lost most of its meaning since there are more institutions available for the elderly and the social pressure against institutionalizing the aged or against the unmarried person is much less severe.

One other factor that has perpetuated a high birth rate

should be noted. It is not related to religious, economic or social motivations for large families, but it is a contributing factor in population growth which must be recognized for what it is. This motivation can be summed up in one word—ego. There are many people who have children for no other reason than for the ego build-up it gives them. They are somehow impressed by the fact that they can reproduce themselves and can see themselves in their children. Even to point out that reproduction is nothing unique—that even the lowest forms of life do it—seems to have little effect upon them. How one changes attitudes of this type remains to be seen.

The large family was the prevailing social pattern until the late nineteenth century. By that time family size was gradually declining, although this is not readily apparent. For those who wished to limit the birth rate prior to that time, several problems were apparent. Contraceptive devices were not as highly developed or as foolproof as today. However, the primary reasons that the family remained large were religious and economic. It also seems safe to assume that the overriding factor was economic, since survival and security, as already explained, were dependent upon large families. This seems particularly apparent when in the late nineteenth century family size declined without any significant change in religious positions. By that time the large family, once an economic asset, had become a liability.

The Industrial Revolution and its impact were the major causes for the change in attitudes toward family size. At the time not many people were aware that the pattern was changing. However, with the vision of hindsight it is now possible to see that the trend began about 1880 and continued until the country was somewhat startled by the time of World War II to discover that the average family size had been drastically reduced. Several factors, some direct and others indirect, were responsible for this change.

With the advent of the Industrial Revolution, the life style of America was dramatically altered, especially for the increasing number of people living in urban environments.

Perhaps one can say that the increasing importance of the city was as significant a factor in reducing the birth rate as any thing else. The worker who now lived in a city and was dependent on a wage system that often fluctuated seasonably was at the mercy of the economic cycle. As an urban dweller, he was removed from the soil where he could usually survive even if the nation were plunged into serious depression. On the farm the machinations of Wall Street or the current status of the international money market had little direct effect upon him. Now, however, his job often depended directly upon these factors, over which he had absolutely no control.

In such an uncertain life style, 'children became a hindrance rather than a benefit. Without the land and its related demands, there was nothing for children to do; they did not produce or add significantly to the family's wealth even if they were able to work at some menial task. At the same time they were economic burdens. They had to be fed and clothed. Some "radicals" were even suggesting the establishment of compulsory education, which would be an added economic drain on the family because of the outright costs involved and the loss of the small incomes that children could earn by selling newspapers, shining shoes, or working in sweatshops. In an urban environment childhood was stretched out to longer and longer periods until some psychologist invented adolescence and thus created a new period of life between childhood and adulthood. Moreover, the child was now subject to more temptations and more likely to get into trouble.

At first children were still important for security reasons. It was not until the 1930s that a system of social security was created to put independence and dignity into old age. Prior to that the harmful effects of the Industrial Revolution and urbanization gradually forced the development of a social consciousness, and some agencies were developed to deal with the new conditions of life. These were often private, humanitarian ventures such as Jane Addams's Hull House in Chicago or church-supported projects stimulated by the appearance of the social gospel in American Protestantism. The emergence of the

Salvation Army and the Christian Science movement were in direct response to the new urban conditions. Yet all of these were private and, to an extent, faltering charities whose reliability was never certain. Likewise, the scope of such agencies was almost always limited by their original founding purposes or by financial considerations. Public agencies were finally created reluctantly to deal with the problems resulting from industrialization and urbanization, but for many years they were scattered and limited in purpose, and very much uncoordinated in their efforts. Since the public commitments were neither solid nor united, the reliability of such agencies was often questionable. The methods of operation of both public and private agencies also made them less than totally effective. Since they were all charitable in nature and dealt with only those in the most desperate conditions, to be forced to depend on their services was often a publicly humiliating and degrading experience. In many social groups there was a serious stigma waiting for one who was aided in such a manner. As a result, it was, still, more self-respecting to depend on one's family for the assistance necessary in old age, illness, or poverty. Thus, the desire for large families continued for much longer than one might have expected.

As the process of urbanization quickened, the census of 1920 revealed that the urban population was larger than the rural for the first time in American history. With a growing consciousness of an urbanized nation and the harmful effects on a major portion of the population, Americans inevitably changed their attitudes toward public charity and large families. Throughout the years the government gradually came to accept more and more social obligations, until the thirties when the New Deal, faced with the massive social impact of the depression, changed the nation into a welfare state, capitalistic society. Since that time the question has not been whether the government will accept more social responsibilities, but what speed and what direction the action will take. Today we have almost reached the point at which there is no social stigma attached to accepting aid or moving to a home for the aged in retirement. Therefore, one of the last emotional attachments to large families has been removed or is in the process of being removed.

One other factor in our population growth and our attitudes toward it is immigration. There seems to be a widely held misconception that America has always been the promised land to the rest of the world and was continually flooded with immigrants from the very beginning. Not true. All Americans, except for the Indians, are immigrants or the children of immigrants, but they did not come continuously or even very early.

During the colonial period there was a fairly steady flow of Europeans, but the number was never excessively large. At the time of the first census in 1790, after 180 years of settlement, the population of the new nation was only about four million. Significant immigration did not begin until the 1840s and 1850s when European conditions, especially in Ireland and Germany, combined with American prosperity, stimulated a larger movement of people across the Atlantic Ocean. In fact, one can follow immigration patterns to America by understanding the economic cycle and the periods of war and peace both in Europe and in the United States. During prosperity and peacetime, the rate of migration rapidly increased, but when times were hard or war existed in either the United States or Europe, the attraction was so much less that immigration almost totally ceased. That trend continued until 1920 when immigration quotas were established and the age of great migration ended.

During its peak immigration received mixed reactions. Some people encouraged it because they saw the benefits to the nation of the foreign population or because labor was needed for the building and development of the industry of this country. Those who were opposed saw the immigrant as a competitor who would depress wages and limit available jobs; others objected because of the different religion, customs, or language of the new immigrants arriving after about 1880 or 1890. The opposition often resulted in rather extreme forms of American nativism.

The opposition to immigration was almost never based on a concern for the size of the population. Foreigners might be opposed for their "popish" ways, for the clannishness they often exhibited, or because of the fear that they would "mongrelize" this country, but even the opponents were often forced to admit grudgingly that they were needed economically. Thus, it would be incorrect to assume that opposition to immigration was ever based on a concern for population control. It is true, however, that immigration, at the time a major source of population growth, was severely restricted just at the time that family sizes were falling and when we had become an urban nation for the first time.

In the twentieth century more concern developed about restricting family size for personal reasons. But early advocates of contraception and family planning had a very rough time of it. Some of them were feminists who met much opposition from men, who saw them as a threat to the established traditions and patterns of life. However, for the professional feminists of the early period, concern about birth control was just one facet of the complex cause they championed.

Gradually the idea of limiting family size became more popular, despite the social and religious opposition it still met. Contraceptive devices became more reliable, making it possible for people to plan the size of their families and the rate at which children would be born. This was, indeed, a major step forward for proponents of population control.

In the post–World War II period, despite the large baby boom in its immediate aftermath, the concern over population became more acute. It became more acceptable for people not to marry and for married couples to decide to forgo having children. Many American Catholics practiced birth control despite the Church's continuing ban on it. Surgical sterilization became safer and more commonly practiced; abortion, long considered immoral and a last resort, became more acceptable among some segments of society. Despite the increased awareness, the birth rate continued to fluctuate.

In recent years a greater concern about population has

been evident. More people have advocated controls, and others have warned us about the immediate dangers of uncontrolled growth. In the very recent past birth control and abortion became a part of the Women's Liberation movement with the demand that women have control over their own bodies and not be subject to the restrictions of a male-dominated society or repressive legislation. Yet, despite the increased concern, the population continued to climb.

The causes are numerous. Some people, believing that the birth control advocates were merely alarmists, ignored the pleas and continued to have babies at their own discretion. Some have said that family size is a matter of personal liberty and have refused adamantly to conform to society's current concerns. Others are still influenced by the older ideas. Another factor not always recognized is that a nation's population will continue to grow even if the birth rate does not change. This is especially true if the number of women coming into the childbearing age is high. This is the geometric progression that Malthus talked about. If a nation reaches Zero Population Growth (ZPG), it takes many years for the population to stabilize at a constant figure. Medical advances reduce infant mortality and stretch life expectancy to a much older age than ever before. Family planning, which some people see as a hopeful sign for population control, is not necessarily a deterrent to population growth. Planning may well mean that the same birth rate will continue, only on a more orderly basis. Family planning does not necessarily encourage individuals to have fewer children; instead, they are encouraged to space them out for the benefit of the mother's health and the family's economic condition.

But, for the supporters of population control there have been at least two recent significant developments. The first is that a report shows the American birth rate to have fallen to ZPG for the first time in our history. This does not mean that our population will be the same next year as it is this year. It means that, if the rate continues to remain static, the American population will level off in forty or fifty years at a much higher total than today. The other development is the recent Supreme Court decision virtually abolishing any legislative restrictions on abortion. Some see this as a great stride forward while others consider it a license for death. The long-range impact of these two developments still remains to be seen.

Before the environmentalist cheers the current situation, he should keep several things in mind. Old ideas die slow deaths. Particularly, the loud heralding of the death of old ideas about population may be premature; it is quite possible that the birth rate could begin to climb again for no discernible reason. There are people who obstinately refuse to see any danger in an increasing population; there are a few who think population control will have a disastrous impact, and, in fact, advocate a higher birth rate. There are always those people also who believe that only the most intelligent people practice birth control while the lower classes proliferate and reduce the overall level of the human species. They think that the more intelligent people should continue to produce large numbers of children for self-protection. They often avoid the touchy question of who decides who will be the judge of intelligence, and they are deaf to the explanations that the higher intelligence group makes greater demands on the environment than any other group. Furthermore, the Church has not surrendered in this struggle.

It is quite possible that the population aspect of the revolution needed to protect the environment has been achieved or is close to it, but it is by no means a certainty. If so, that is one part of the battle already won. However, vigilance is always a necessity.

7

THE FUTURE REVOLUTION

The present state of the environment is the result of many forces; our actions toward nature reflect the complexity of modern life. It is not necessary to isolate specific causes of a particular destructive act; instead, we must realize that our current practices are a result of the totality of each individual's experience. In the same fashion, a nation's attitudes are a mixture of individual attitudes and experiences and the nation's place in the world, its national history, and its concept and practice of nationalism.

In the United States, as in all the world, one must realize that the present precarious condition of nature is the result of our historical development. As has been shown, attitudes and actions toward the environment which seemed insignificant or inconsequential two or three hundred years ago, or even just a short time ago, have developed into major problems today. The consequences of our actions, unfortunately, seem to increase geometrically, just as Malthus explained the growth of population. Where the indiscriminate cutting of trees by one pioneer family had little impact on nature, the problem multiplied as hundreds or thousands of families did the same thing. Even then, however, the impact was still not so serious that it could not be tolerated. But when the actions of isolated groups began to overlap one another, the problems became much more apparent.

Therefore, by the early twentieth century a few far-seeing individuals became alarmed about the ultimate result of the public's indifference toward nature. As the years of the twentieth century passed, the condition of nature became apparent even to the most casual observer. It no longer required a specialist, a scientist, or a technician to realize what was happening. In everyday life individuals were able to witness the unclean air, the dirty rivers and streams, and the accumulating junk all around them. When they stopped to ask what was happening and why, far too many people had absolutely no understanding of what was wrong. Some observers went so far as to say that the ignorance thus expressed was the result of an American death wish that refused to recognize the reality of what was happening.

The need to understand this almost lemming-like phenomenon became more pressing. Scientists warned us of the consequences of our acts, and social scientists began to devise means to change the behavior patterns responsible for the destruction. Unfortunately, their suggestions are only a part of the answer. Truly, if improvement is to come, scientific and technological knowledge of the problem and of proposed solutions will be needed. But at the same time efforts at change will meet many obstacles if there is little understanding of the origins of the attitudes that create, or at least permit, such ecological destruction. The past must be understood as a major contributing factor in the destruction of nature.

In truth, the problems which have reached crisis proportions in the mid-twentieth century are merely the result of attitudes and actions prevalent for the past 350 years. The more immediate crisis of the past twenty years is the result of an intensification of the overall attitudes. Undoubtedly, unless actions are changed, the problems will become more serious, and, if predictions are correct, man's future on the earth will be severely restricted.

Therefore, if man has any sincere hope of changing the future for the better, he must understand the past before it is too late. Moreover, the problem is, to a large degree, the immediate responsibility of the Western world. With the exception of population pressures, virtually every cause of environmental destruction is most serious in the industrialized West. As was described earlier, even the population crisis is as much the fault of the smaller industrialized West as it is of the heavily populated underdeveloped countries where each individual places less burden on the environment than does his counterpart in western Europe or the United States.

If one concludes, as he eventually must, that the world faces a crisis of unprecedented proportions, he may legitimately ask what the answer is. Unfortunately, there is no clear-cut, definitive answer. One could say that all destructive acts toward nature should be immediately terminated. That certainly would be one solution, but it would create more problems than it solved. It would completely destroy the present economic, political, and social systems of the world. There is nothing particularly sacred about the present social order, but the chaos that would result from immediate and complete change would be so serious that few would like to contemplate it. How to protect the environment for the use of ourselves and our posterity without destroying the benefits of modern society is the dilemma the world faces today. Without being overly pessimistic, some might conclude that it would take a Solomon to devise a workable answer, and possibly even he would be unable to do it.

If one limits himself, as we have done here, to an analysis of the American experience and the environmental crisis of today, he faces one other problem of significant proportions that has not been previously discussed. The American has been, historically, one who seeks quick and simple solutions to the problems that hinder his rapid movement toward his goals. He has not been one to philosophize about the universe and to see the world as a complex interaction of various forces that require subtle and sensitive reactions. The American sees the world in absolutes—in blacks and whites with no gray area in between.

When confronted in the past with an issue of significance, the American's most automatic reaction was to ignore it as long as possible. When its existence could no longer be denied, he suddenly attacked it with a vigor and determination designed to end the disruption of his normal activity as rapidly as possible. He usually moved in the most direct fashion to eliminate the problem. In the twentieth century the most common method of solution was to seek legislative action. Unfortunately, the problem was often too complex and too deep-rooted to be solved in such a simple, direct fashion. After a relatively short period of attempting change, the American usually became weary of the struggle and his interest began to wane. In most cases, his interests very quickly turned to other things, and the reformist impulse and energy shifted to other activities.

The examples in American history of this attitude are so numerous that a discussion of them would, in effect, be a recounting of American history. A few can serve, however, as points of illumination. The most recent example is the civil rights movement. The problem of racial equality was ignored by the white community for over a hundred years until it reached crisis proportions. Then many Americans were astounded to discover the inequities in the American system. Spurred by their consciences, they moved quickly to eliminate the discrimination in what was considered the fastest and most simple fashion—federal legislation. When massive federal involvement proved not to be the whole answer and when the complexities of a plural society became more apparent, numerous Americans quickly developed an attitude that assumed that the problem no longer existed. Hoping to avoid the issue, they decided that the federal legislation had eliminated racial discrimination and that black people had achieved equality. The folly of this view was obvious. Others placed the blame for the failure of federal legislation on blacks themselves because of the growing Black Power movement and the new exclusiveness in the black community. For whatever reason, the support for civil rights activity declined precipitately as soon as a quick and simple solution could not be found.

Of course, a careful examination of the situation reveals that the issue did not lend itself to simple answers. The racial and ethnic divisions in American society go so deep that simple solutions are not really possible; many people were shocked to realize the depth of the antagonism and the apparent fallacy of the "melting pot" theory, a myth that had sustained generations of white Americans. American impatience was also evident in the unwillingness to grapple with the real issue and to maintain a long-term devotion to the cause.

The simplistic, legalistic approach to problem solving in American history was also evident in the Prohibition movement. By the time of the first World War, efforts over the past century convinced more people than ever before that the heavy consumption of alcohol had created serious social problems. The result was the imposition of legal prohibition. Unfortunately, too few of the reformers took serious note of what its consequences might be. They seemed to think that a centuries-old habit could be abolished overnight by simply making it illegal. They also seemed to be unaware that the program had overtones of class legislation. This became especially apparent during the attempts to enforce the law. The wealthy and prominent citizen who wished to drink could usually still do so with only a minimum amount of discomfort. He could still obtain the better quality beverages if he had the money to pay for them or if he knew the right people. This option was denied to most average people, who were then forced either to abstain, to purchase liquor of poor or questionable quality from bootleggers, or to make their own beverage despite the health risks involved. Moreover, prohibitionists attacked their opponents with a vigorous crusading spirit that was often rude, patronizing, and condescending. It has been suggested that the prohibitionists may have done more harm than good by their tactics.

Unquestionably, the American has sought simple and speedy solutions to his problems, although the problems have very seldom been of such a nature that they would readily respond to quick treatment. Environmental protection is an issue that is so complex and so interwined with the past that it, too, will not be solved by simplistic solutions or rapid action.

Another American attitude that is reflected by the Prohibition movement, among others, is the insensitivity to the wishes of others. American reformers plunged into movements that they concluded were necessary with a kind of bullheaded determination to end the problem as soon as possible with little concern about the desires or motivation of those who opposed them. Then they very often wrapped themselves in moralistic or patriotic rhetoric which they hoped would give them immunity to criticism.

Again, the examples are very numerous. Few civil rights activists were interested in the attitudes of southerners or others who opposed racial integration. Instead, such opponents were branded at best as reactionaries who did not want change or at worst as racists, bigots, or hypocrites. Opponents of the Vietnam war characterized those who supported American policy as warmongers, imperialists, or baby-killers. Opponents of Prohibition were accused of being degenerates or immoral people. The list could continue indefinitely. Obviously, when reformers use such tactics, they place their opponents on the defensive even to the point of supporting positions that they might not normally endorse. Then, of course, when and if the reformers succeed in their objectives, they often find themselves faced with a sullen, uncooperative public that puts up more resistance in the future. As a result, the achievement of the reformers' goals is often undermined even after they have apparently achieved victory. The tactics of the reformers, therefore, are just as important as are their ultimate objectives.

This is not to assume that the reformers themselves are
not attacked by their opponents. They are often branded as
anarchists, degenerates, permissive, or unpatriotic. The abuse
that they may receive is one of the risks that a reformer must
take. But, at the same time, one is tempted to wonder how
much of this vilification is prompted by the tactics of the reformers themselves. The other thing to remember is that it
is the reformer who is challenging the status quo and asking
for change that may lead to all sorts of consequences. It is
only reasonable to assume that anyone who has his normal
patterns of action challenged will resort to an emotional and
sometimes irrational reaction. The reformer must recognize
this and expect it to happen or, better yet, his efforts to bring
change should take cognizance of what he is asking of people,
and his tactics should be planned to avoid as much acrimony
and bitterness as possible.

The environmentalist faces all these ingrained American
characteristics. If he does not at least take them into account
when planning his actions, he seems doomed to disappoint-
ment. Above all, he must be aware of the historical context
from which a propensity for environmental destruction developed. Without that awareness, he would seem to be doing
little more than tilting at windmills. To change attitudes that
have been acceptable for the indefinite past, the reformer, the
environmentalist included, must find the root causes and work
to change them. Obviously, without those deep-seated antecedents the problem would never have occurred. For example,
if he can convince the public that the once admired virtue of
large families is no longer necessary in a developed country,
then the public will probably restrict family size voluntarily
without outside pressure and without the public judgment
that large families are socially destructive. If he can convince the public that the idea of progress as normally defined
has fulfilled its purpose through a normal life span and that
it must now be redefined, then half the battle is won. With
a redefinition of the concept, it is very possible that a consensus will develop that progress does not necessarily mean

an evergrowing GNP or a new model of automobile every year. With breakthroughs such as these, the problems of the environment will disappear.

But the warning must be made again. To attack people for beliefs they hold will not necessarily win them over; the reverse will probably be true. Where they were once only lukewarm defenders of high birth rates or a continually rising GNP, they may become avid supporters if somehow their integrity is questioned by those attempting change.

Another obstacle which faces the environmentalist, as is true with any reformer, is the age-old problem of public apathy. Generally speaking, the public does not become agitated about public issues unless it is directly and personally affected. No matter how much people decry public indifference, it is fairly easy to understand. Most people are too involved in their daily activities to be overly concerned about issues in which they feel no direct personal involvement. Ironically, many of those who condemn and make a big issue of public apathy are themselves often guilty of some of the worst apathy about other things.

The environmentalist, if he is to have real hope of success, must somehow develop a program and method that will keep his issue before the public in a constant and enduring fashion. A temporary slackening of the public relations side of the program can easily result in large blocks of people drifting away from a movement.

Again, it is important to state that there is no simple, easy solution to the problem of environmental destruction. Moreover, that is not the purpose of this book. There are probably many ways to approach the issue. The two indispensable tools necessary, however, are a technological-scientific knowledge of what is specifically wrong and an understanding of how and why we got where we are today.

The environmentalist must, of course, be truly aware of what he is asking of the American people—revolution. True, we as a nation were born in revolution, and we have given much lip service to the concept in the years since, but our national history reveals that we have not been quite so devoted to revolution as we would like to think or as we would like others to believe. Therefore, when a reformer asks for revolution, he must be prepared for the consequences of his suggestion.

Finally, of course, the environmentalist must be aware of his tactics and their consequences. He seems to have two, or possibly three, alternatives. On the one hand, he can conclude that the crisis is so serious that he must charge full-steam ahead and accept the resulting animosity and resistance to his goals. On the other hand, he can give up in despair of any hope of salvaging the environment and let the results come as they may. The more reasonable approach would seem to be an attitude that is fully aware of the crisis but which also accepts and understands the reluctance of people to make sweeping changes. With patience, understanding, firmness, and commitment to his goals, the environmentalist just might be able to save nature for the use of our children and grandchildren.

NOTES

CHAPTER 1

1. Page Smith, *The Historian and History* (rpt., New York: Vintage Books, 1964), p. 226.

2. Ibid., passim.

CHAPTER 2

1. Eric Hoffer, *The True Believer* (rpt., New York: Time Books, 1963), p. 30.

2. Ibid., p. 11.

3. Ibid., p. 7.

4. For an excellent discussion of this question, see the introduction to Bernard Sternsher, *Hitting Home; The Great Depression in Town and Country* (Chicago: Quadrangle Books, 1970).

5. Oscar Handlin, *The Uprooted* (rpt., New York: Grosset's Universal Library, 1951).

6. Frederick Jackson Turner, "The Significance of the Frontier in American History," American Historical Association *Annual Report,* 1893.

7. Richard Hofstadter, *Anti-Intellectualism in American Life* (New York: Alfred A. Knopf, 1963).

8. *New York Times,* July 30, 1968.

9. Ibid., September 8, 1968.

10. Ibid., September 26, 1968.

11. Ibid., October 8, 1968.

12. Ibid., October 20, 1969.

13. Ibid., October 31, 1969.

CHAPTER 3

1. Robert Ardrey, *The Territorial Imperative* (New York: Atheneum, 1966).

2. Ardrey, *African Genesis: A Personal Investigation into the Animal Origins and Nature of Man* (New York: Atheneum, 1961).

3. Richard J. Walton, *Cold War and Counter-Revolution: The Foreign Policy of John F. Kennedy* (New York: Viking, 1972), p. 23.

4. Ibid.

5. Paul R. Ehrlich, *The Population Bomb* (New York: Ballantine, 1968).

CHAPTER 4

1. Leo E. Oliva, "Our Frontier Heritage and the Environment," *The American West* 9 (January, 1972), 44–47, 61–63.

2. As quoted ibid., 62.

3. Ibid.

4. Ibid.

5. Ibid.

6. Stewart S. Cort, "Truth—and Consequences," *New York Times,* August 30, 1972.

7. Hofstadter, *The Age of Reform* (rpt., New York: Vintage Books, 1955).

CHAPTER 5

1. Cyril Northcote Parkinson, *Parkinson's Law* (Boston: Houghton Mifflin, 1957).

2. See, for example, G. William Domhoff, *The Higher Circles: The Governing Class in America* (New York: Random House, 1970).

3. Adam Smith, *An Inquiry into the Nature and Causes of the Wealth of Nations* (rpt., New York: Modern Library, 1937).

4. *Louisville* (Kentucky) *Times,* February 6, 1973; John Ed Pearce, "The Red River Gorge," *Courier-Journal & Times Magazine* (Louisville, Kentucky), September 7, 1969.

5. *Texas Observer,* August 1, 1969, p. 12.

6. Ibid., p. 14.

7. Ibid., p. 16.

8. *The Texas Observer* has provided a continuing coverage of this issue for several years.

9. *The Texas Observer,* January 19, 1973, pp. 10–11.

10. As quoted ibid., p. 11.

CHAPTER 6

1. See Ehrlich, *The Population Bomb,* passim.

2. Thomas Robert Malthus, *On Population* (rpt., New York: Modern Library, 1960), passim.

3. David Ricardo, *The Principles of Political Economy and Taxation* (New York: E. P. Dutton, 1911), passim.

4. See, for example, Barry Commoner, "Can We Survive?" *Washington Monthly* 1 (December, 1969), 12–21, reprinted in Leonard Freedman, ed., *Issues of the Seventies* (Belmont, California: Wadsworth Publishing Co., 1970), pp. 165–177.

INDEX

134